# Hands of Faith

# HANDS of FAITH

*A Historical and Theological Study of the Two Kinds*
*of Righteousness in Lutheran Thought*

## Jordan Cooper

Foreword by Joel Biermann

WIPF & STOCK · Eugene, Oregon

HANDS OF FAITH
A Historical and Theological Study of the Two Kinds of Righteousness in Lutheran
Thought

Wipf & Stock
An Imprint of Wipf and Stock Publishers
199 W. 8th Ave., Suite 3
Eugene, OR 97401

www.wipfandstock.com

PAPERBACK ISBN: 978-1-4982-3593-8
HARDCOVER ISBN: 978-1-4982-3595-2
EBOOK ISBN: 978-1-4982-3594-5

Manufactured in the U.S.A.                                        06/02/16

The book is dedicated to my parents, through whom I was trained as a child in Christian virtue and obedience to the commands of God.

# Contents

*Foreword by Joel Biermann* | ix

Diagnosing the Problem: Why This Study Is Important | 1
Two Kinds of Righteousness: Three Proposals | 11
Two Kinds of Righteousness in Luther's Theology | 37
The Two Kinds of Righteousness in the Lutheran Confessions | 63
The Two Kinds of Righteousness in Lutheran Orthodoxy | 88
Conclusion | 113

Appendix: Two Kinds of Righteousness in Scripture | 135

*Bibliography* | 153

# Foreword

There was a time when theology was considered the queen of the sciences. Earlier generations conceived of nothing greater than God; *ipso facto*, the study of God was the pinnacle of all human knowing, or as formerly referenced, science. And while what typically comes to mind when one hears the word "science" may have evolved since the time when nearly everyone accepted the aphorism, in very real way, the idea still holds. This is not to say that theology is the most intellectually demanding pursuit known to man. Indeed, that argument would convince few. There are branches of the hard sciences that make extraordinary cognitive demands on those who seek to master them—demands that may well exceed what is necessary for the work of theology. But, that precisely is the crux. There is no mastering theology, and those who would pursue the study of divinity are compelled to confront continually the hard truth of what they do not and cannot know about the focus of their study. In his inimitable and self-deprecating way, Stanley Hauerwas puts it well: "Theology is a discipline whose subject should always put in doubt the very idea that those who practice it know what they are doing."[1] In theology, we know only what our subject gives us to know. The theological "scientist" does not experiment, hypothesize, or discover anything about God—all of the typical verbiage notwithstanding. He merely confesses what he has been given to confess.

For the theologian, the greatest challenge is learning to confess faithfully and well—coupled, of course, with the enduring challenge of reining in the curiosity and pride that seek always to treat theology as one more rational pursuit, a field of play for the display of intellectual prowess. The requisite virtues are many, and none painlessly achieved or retained. Faithful confession is confession that aligns with the church's confession.

---

1. Hauerwas, *Hannah's Child*, ix.

Innovation is never the goal. As any careful reading of the Book of Concord makes plain, this was ideal at the time of Luther and Melanchthon as well as in the days of Chemnitz and Andreä. It should be our ideal today. What the church has been given, we confess—and with confident assurance. Yet, even our most confident assertions are couched in a sense of wonder and awe palpably conscious that we are speaking of God, who defies all human definition and comprehension. And our assertions are, or should be, further tempered by an awareness of the fact that within the living body of Christ, there are myriad expressions of God's truth that are faithful to what has been given. Manifest in an assortment of traditions and schools of thoughts, however, the church is distressingly prone to a narrow parochialism that bears more resemblance to the artificial allegiances we accord competing athletic franchises than to the corporate diversity and unity that is the body of Christ. All this is to say that I am grateful for the work of faithful theologians who forthrightly speak God's truth, and sometimes do so in ways unfamiliar, strange, and even disconcerting to my ears, and yet wholly within the church's confession. Which is to say, I am grateful for the work of Jordan Cooper.

Of course the language and discourse common to Cooper's expression of truth is hardly that discordant with my own ways of expression. We both are willingly and freely constrained by a common confession and a peculiar heritage within the body of the church. More remarkably than that, we are even linked by our mutual appreciation for the two kinds of righteousness as a dynamic and effective means of expressing God's truth in the contemporary context. This, it turns out, is not universally true of all who join us in our heritage and confession. Perhaps this text will help to remedy what is, to my mind, an unnecessary and somewhat reactionary repudiation of the two kinds of righteousness by some who are fellow heirs of Luther. Still, even with much common ground, Cooper brings emphases and nuances that are not my own, and so he forces me, and probably other readers as well, to think again . . . not so much about what is being confessed but rather how it is confessed. A theologian should always be eager to improve on his own expression of God's truth, of course; and the endlessly changing cultural context of those who listen to our confession warrants a willingness to entertain and even embrace fresh ways of communicating God's truth. I doubt that I will ever be one to speak often and enthusiastically about the mystical union, and I am virtually certain that I will never describe the work of God's Spirit in the believer as some sort of ontological union. Nevertheless, I can see Cooper's point in doing so, and will not begrudge him the latitude to confess God's timeless truth in ways unfamiliar to my own ears. Not being particularly prescient, I may even surprise myself and one day find that my context demands a shift in expression and the use of terms and phrases that are today more than a little uncomfortable. Such is the work of a theologian who speaks God's truth as faithfully and as convincingly as possible—thus in ways that are contextually variable, yet invariably deferential and unassuming.

The book that follows ably presents a lucid portrait of the dynamic interaction that is the two kinds of righteousness. Another voice concurring with the foundational role of this duality in early Lutheran thinking is a gift in itself. Cooper provides further service by tracing the use of the distinction between the two kinds of righteousness down through later generations of Lutheran writers and teachers. This is valuable work and further substantiates both the legitimacy and the remarkable usefulness of the recognition and distinction of two kinds of righteousness. It is no surprise that one who is currently serving God's people in a living parish so readily recognizes the gift that Luther has left his progeny by explicating and practicing the distinction between the two kinds of righteousness. Accordingly, Cooper is acutely aware of the needs of parish pastors and so offers concrete and applicable insights into the immediate impact of the two kinds of righteousness on the tasks of gospel proclamation and the daily care of God's flock. A book that furthers such vital work deserves reading.

Joel Biermann
Epiphanytide, 2015

# Diagnosing the Problem
## Why This Study Is Important

Since the time of the Reformation, the Lutheran church has been accused of incipient antinomianism due to its emphasis on justification by grace alone, through faith alone, on account of Christ alone. It was the charge of Roman polemicists in the sixteenth century that Luther's doctrine of justification would eventually lead to licentious living and the abuse of Christian liberty. Though Lutheran theologians have continued, through the centuries, to emphasize the necessity and the role of good works within the Christian's life, these charges have remained. In recent years, some Lutherans have accepted the caricature as their own, donning T-shirts with the phrase "weak on sanctification" plastered on the front. This gives further credence to the old complaints that Lutherans ignore the reality of sanctified living.

Since the decline of Pietism in the nineteenth century, Lutherans have feared conflating law and gospel, and making assurance of one's justification depend upon good works or an experience of grace, rather than upon the objective work of Christ for the salvation of sinners.[1] While avoiding legalism is a laudable goal, attempts to distance the Lutheran Reformation from the Pietist movement have sometimes led to a new form of antinomianism. If one views legalism as the ultimate enemy, without any concern for the real danger of ignoring the importance of Christian living, then such antinomianism is the inevitable result. Contemporary Lutheranism has—in many cases—been reduced to a theology that emphasizes justification to the exclusion of sanctification, and to an unreasonable emphasis on the law-gospel schema, to the exclusion of proper exegesis in preaching and other theological pursuits.

1. See Forde, "Justification," in Braaten, *Christian Dogmatics* II:399–424.

1

The solution to this dilemma is to recapture the historic Lutheran distinction between the two kinds of righteousness: active, and passive. The passive righteousness of faith in justification is determinative for the divine-human relationship, and this fact distinguishes Luther from his medieval forebears. This does not, however, negate the importance of the Christian's active life of obedience under God's law. This reality, often terms "sanctification," is an essential teaching of the Christian faith which is an important factor of historic Lutheran theology.

## What to Expect in This Work

There have been several essays and books in recent years which have touched on the theme of the two kinds of righteousness, but there have not been many book-length treatments of the subject. This work is an attempt to provide a framework for the two kinds of righteousness by utilizing the writings of Luther, the confessional documents in Lutheranism, and classical Lutheran theologians. Drawing upon previous research and writing on the subject, I hope to provide a full and consistently Lutheran framework in which we can proclaim the necessity of both faith and works.

In my previous writings, I have sought to counter some of the problematic movements within contemporary Lutheran theology, and this volume draws upon the conclusions reached in that previous research. In *The Righteousness of One: An Evaluation of Early Patristic Soteriology in Light of the New Perspective on Paul*, I sought to challenge the common characterizations of Luther as a forensic-only theologian by demonstrating continuity between Luther and the church fathers in teaching both forensic justification and participationist soteriological motifs. In my book *Christification: A Lutheran Approach to Theosis*, I expounded upon the theme of theosis, demonstrating that there is a Lutheran manner in which one can utilize theosis terminology which is consistent with the Patristic sources, Scripture, and the Lutheran theological tradition. In some ways, this is an expansion of those two works, as I continue to offer a proposal for a Lutheranism that is genuinely catholic and which avoids reductionistic caricatures. As I have continued to study the distinction between the two kinds of righteousness, I have also revised my manner of speaking in some ways to bring further clarity to my previous writings. For example, in my work *The Righteousness of One*, I did not strongly distinguish between the *unio fidei formalis* and the *unio mystica*.[2] The distinction between the two kinds of righteousness has helped me as a theologian to nuance and strengthen various theological categories, especially by more sharply distinguishing passive righteousness and the indwelling and sanctifying work of the Holy Spirit (active righteousness), while maintaining the essential connection between justification and sanctification. The work of the theologian is always one of growth and sometimes revision.

In my previous work, I define the idea of Christification as

> The ontological[3] union of God and man, initiated through the incarnation, which the Christian partakes in through faith. Through this union, that which belongs properly to Christ—namely divine incorruptibility and immortality—is transferred to the believer by faith. This union is increased and strengthened as the Christian participates in the sacramental life of the church, and it is demonstrated through growth in personal holiness.[4]

Conformity to the image of Christ through one's mystical union with God fits well within the two-kinds-of-righteousness framework, explaining how the good works of the Christian are performed, and explicating the difference between the civic righteousness of the unbeliever and the inchoate righteousness of the Christian. The two-kinds-of-righteousness distinction allows one to speak both forensically and ontologically without conflating the important distinction between these two soteriological categories.

This book begins with first analyzing some of the important work on the subject of the two kinds of righteousness that has been written in the last century. I then expound upon the subject of the two kinds of righteousness within Luther's own thought and demonstrate that it is a consistent theme throughout his career, though his terminology sometimes differs

2. These concepts will be expounded below. The *unio fidei formalis* is the formal union of faith whereby one is placed into Christ. The *unio mystica* is the indwelling of Christ.

3. The term "ontological" is quite fluid and thus deserves some explanation. By "ontological" I do not mean that one's human substance is somehow transformed into a non-human or divine substance. Man's essential being remains the same. In this way, the regenerative changes within the Christian are accidental. In other words, regeneration and sanctification radically change the human person while he still remains, in essence, the same human person. The being of man and the being of God are united, though this union does not in any way involve a transformation of one into the other. God himself dwells within and unites himself with the human creature. It is in this sense that such a union is "ontological." It is a union of two persons, and thus two substances.

4. Cooper, *Christification*, 19.

from contemporary proposals. I also examine the Lutheran confessional documents and explicate the relationship between faith and works as consistent with the two-kinds-of-righteousness distinction. Finally, I examine the theme of the two kinds of righteousness in the historic Lutheran tradition, showing that even if the exact terminology is not utilized, this distinction is taught by various scholastic Lutheran theologians in the history of the church.

The goal of this work is fourfold: first, I hope to demonstrate that the theme of the two kinds of righteousness is not a novel development within Lutheran theology. Instead, it is inherent in the historic Lutheran tradition, extending from Luther's theology, through the confessional documents, to the scholastic tradition. Second, the Lutheran tradition has never been antinomian; there is a consistent emphasis on ethical formation, love, and obedience to God's law throughout the history of the Lutheran church. Third, there is an intimate connection between union with Christ and the two kinds of righteousness. The believer participates in a legal union with Christ by faith, and in this union, receives the righteousness of Christ. This is an important facet of passive righteousness which is not often discussed in contemporary literature on the subject. In terms of active righteousness, there is a second type of union wherein Christ dwells within the believer, progressively forming the believer in his own image. Finally, the theme of eucharistic sacrifice will be explored as a means to explicate the nature of the first table of God's law. In contemporary approaches to active righteousness, the good works of the believer are explained solely as a horizontal reality. While this formulation is beneficial as an explanation of the difference between the human-human and the divine-human relationships, it fails to give a sufficient explanation of the love which the believer is called to express toward God. Throughout the work, it is made clear that the historic Lutheran tradition has emphasized piety toward God, though not as a reality which establishes or increases divine love toward the sinner. Instead, this love toward God is an act of thanksgiving in response to divine initiative in salvation.

## Law-Gospel Reductionism

Twentieth-century theology was highly influenced by existential philosophy. Many of the figures involved in the crisis theology arising in the 1920s and 1930s utilized the works of Kierkegaard, Heidegger, and others associated with existential philosophy. Rudolph Bultmann, for example, used the philosophy of Neo-Kantianism alongside the categories of Martin Heidegger to formulate an approach to the Christian faith that was devoid of myth[5] and centered on the personal encounter that God has with man, wherein one is led to an open future.[6] For Bultmann, theology is simply about an event—the event of God's act upon the sinner, and the sinner's moment of existential decision. Similarly, Barth and Brunner argued that the word of God itself is an event, only becoming God's word in the I-Thou encounter with the sinner.[7] Scripture is not *objectively* the word of God, but it *becomes* the word of God.[8] This prioritization of event over objective being and content influenced a number of Lutheran thinkers who sought to explain the distinction between law and gospel within Luther's theology.

Within an existential framework, the law of God is described not as God's eternal will as it was in traditional Lutheran orthodoxy, but instead as something which acts upon the sinner. Werner Elert exemplifies this tradition, emphasizing the law as that which "makes us guilty. It accuses, damns, kills. It makes the heart a hell and confirms for us that the primal experience (*Urerlebnis*) takes place with the cooperation of God."[9] For Lutheran orthodoxy, the law is the objective will of God which corresponds to his own character.[10] The commandments serve three functions: to curb sin, to show one the reality of sin and consequently drive them to Christ, and finally as a guide in Christian living.[11] If the law is defined primarily not by what it *is*, but by what it *does*, then the third function of the law essentially has no purpose. The law is not an objective norm to be obeyed, but an

5. This is explained in Bultmann's work "New Testament and Mythology," which can be found in Bartsch, *Kerygma and Myth*.

6. For more on Bultmann and Heidegger, see Macquarrie, *Existentialist Theology*. The influence of Neo-Kantian writers on Bultmann's thought has been catalogued in Dennison, *Young Bultmann*.

7. The "I-Thou" language is utilized heavily by Brunner, drawing on Martin Buber's book *I and Thou*.

8. See Barth, *Word of God*.

9. Elert, *Structure of Lutheranism*, 37.

10. See Schmid, *Doctrinal Theology*, 508–20.

11. However, some Lutheran theologians have divided the second use up into two separate uses, thus holding to a fourfold use of the law. Hollaz distinguishes between the elenchtical (to show sin) and pedagogical (to lead one to Christ) uses of the law (Schmid, *Doctrinal Theology*, 515–16).

existential reality which acts upon the sinner.[12] Werner Elert, William Lazareth, and several other twentieth-century theologians argued that Lutheran theology is distinct from the Reformed tradition due to its rejection of the third use of the law.[13]

This trend, sometimes described as "law-gospel reductionism," is exemplified in the Radical Lutheran school of thought promoted by the late Gerhard Forde.[14] In contradistinction to traditional scholastic Lutheranism, Forde argues that "Law is defined not only as a specific set of demands as such, but rather in terms of what it does to you."[15] The law is not the eternal will of God—eternal in its essence and in conformity with God's nature.[16] Rather, the law is defined by its effect, by what it does to the hearer. If this is the case, the law is then defined not as the good will of God, but as that which accuses. This is the inevitable result of failing to distinguish between the *opera Dei* (works of God), and the *verba Dei* (words of God). In traditional Lutheranism, accusation is one *function* of the law, but it does not *define* the law. The terms "law" and "gospel" are sometimes used as shorthand to refer to God's acts of killing and making alive (which is a perfectly valid thing to do in the appropriate context); but in a more proper sense, they simply refer to the two manners in which God speaks, rather than two separate existential realities. In the prelapsarian state, for example, the law served only a positive purpose, guiding Adam and Eve to live in God's will. In the same manner, God's law still serves a positive function in guiding the Christian in obedience to God's will.

For Radical Lutherans, the existential reality of God's speech does not only refer to the law, but also to the gospel. Forde contends that "the gospel too, is defined primarily by what it does: the gospel comforts because it puts

---

12. Arand and Biermann write, "Perhaps as an overreaction to Barth, a number of Lutheran theologians transformed the Lutheran dictum *lex semper accusat* into *lex sole accusat*. It was assumed and asserted that the Law cannot guide because it only accuses. The distinction between Law and Gospel became an opposition in which the Gospel triumphs over not only the wrath of God but over the Law itself" (Arand, "Why the Two Kinds," 124).

13. This history is explained extensively in Murray, *Law, Life, and the Living God*.

14. The name "Radical Lutheranism" comes from an article of that title by Gerhard Forde which can be found in Forde, *More Radical Gospel*, 3–16.

15. Forde, *Where God Meets Man*, 15.

16. "That is why Luther did not speak of law as something static and unchangeable. Laws will and must change in their form as the times demand" (ibid., 111).

an end to the voice of the law."[17] Traditional scholastic Lutheranism defined the gospel as an explicit set of propositions about the objective work of Christ in history.[18] The gospel certainly does do something to the hearer, as God works the *vocatio* through the preached word, but the gospel is not defined by its effect. By promoting the effect of the gospel over the content of the gospel, Forde contends that the *effects* of God's speech are more central than the *content* of that speech.[19] When the law and the gospel are defined not by what they *are*, but by what they *do*, then they are approached as two contradictory aspects of God, who speaks contrary words. Oswald Bayer, for example, writes, "The gospel is not a general idea, but a concrete word that addresses a specific person in a particular situation. For the gospel, in its precise sense, is the word with which the triune God himself appears before me, defends me against his own accusing law, and intercedes for me."[20] The law and the gospel are viewed as a polarity rather than complementary words. The gospel, then, is not only victory over sin, but over the law itself. Bayer even confesses, "God is not consistent but contradicts himself. Here we see God against God!"[21] According to Paulson, the Lutheran tradition was wrong for emphasizing an ultimate unity between law and gospel. He argues, "In order to defend the necessity of the chief article of justification by faith alone, they had recourse to the eternal law and sought an ultimate unity of law and gospel that would enable this order of salvation to be accomplished."[22] Law-gospel reductionism fails to understand the unity of God himself, and particularly the unity in his two modes of speaking, by adopting an existential approach to the doctrines of law and gospel.

The law-gospel reductionism of this movement within Lutheran theology also promotes a justification-only reductionism. All of the redemptive benefits of God are encapsulated by God's justifying word. This leaves no place for discussions of regeneration and sanctification that expound inherent, rather than imputed, righteousness. Oswald Bayer argues that there is no essential difference between justification and sanctification: "When, nevertheless, Luther speaks about 'sanctification' he simply talks

17. Ibid., 16.

18. Hollaz writes that most specifically, the gospel is "the work of Christ already manifested in history" (as cited in Schmid, *Doctrinal Theology*, 517).

19. Forde, *Where God Meets Man*, 16.

20. Bayer, *Theology the Lutheran Way*, 123.

21. Ibid., 104.

22. Paulson, *Lutheran Theology*, 12.

about justification. Justification and sanctification are not for him two separate acts that we can distinguish, as though sanctification follows after justification, and has to do so."[23] While traditional Lutheran theology holds that justification and sanctification are two separate, but connected, events in the *ordo salutis*, Bayer conflates both into one act of justification. The idea of progress, in the moral sense, is rejected as an abandonment of the chief article.[24] Forde contends: "The 'progress' of the Christian, therefore, is the progress of one who has constantly to get used to the fact that we are justified totally by faith, constantly has somehow to 'recover,' so to speak, from that death blow to pride and presumption—or better, is constantly being raised from the tomb of all pious ambition to something quite new."[25] Growth in the Christian faith is limited to one's growth in understanding justification, rather than actual progress in virtue. It is simply becoming less moralistic, and more gospel-focused.

The concept of virtue itself is rejected in the Radical Lutheran movement. Paulson argues that "virtue is our problem. Religion is not given for morality; it is there to end it."[26] The search for virtue is seen as a moralistic enterprise which negates the importance of divine imputation. Paulson further writes, "Christian faith is not moving toward virtue, it is taking leave of it."[27] He is extremely critical of traditional Lutheran scholastic categories which, he purports, deviate from Luther's gospel-centric theology. For example, Paulson rejects the distinction between the two powers of faith, whereby the Christian, by faith, is both receptive before God in justification and active in the world through sanctification. He argues:

> Even the scholastic, orthodox Lutherans of the seventeenth century (against whom these "new Lutherans" were speaking) fell into this problem with technical distinctions they introduced into

23. Bayer, *Living by Faith*, 59.

24. Forde similarly writes: "Sanctification cannot, therefore, mean that the ideas of moral progress blasted by divine imputation of righteousness are now subtly smuggled back in under the table. The sin to be removed is precisely such understandings of progress. The justification is not a mere beginning point which can somehow be allowed to recede into the background while the supposed 'real' business of sanctification takes front and center. The unconditional justification is the perpetual fountain, the constant source of whatever 'righteousness' we may acquire. 'Complete' sanctification is not the goal but the source of all good works" (Forde, *Justification by Faith*, 51).

25. Ibid., 51.

26. Paulson, *Lutheran Theology*, 2.

27. Ibid., 3.

justification like two "energies" of faith (passive and active), one receiving Christ's merit, the other the power to love. These sturdy theologians in the century following Luther fell to the temptation of the great teacher Melanchthon, allowing themselves to be drawn back into the legal scheme in terms of Aristotle's categories of cause and effect. Whether one makes faith a cause of justification or an effect of it, the heart of Christ and the preacher's word are removed so that only a carcass remains.[28]

For Paulson, traditional Lutheran categories are part of the "legal scheme" that he eschews as opposed to the gospel.

The proponents of the Radical Lutheran approach to theology are to be praised for their emphasis on divine grace in opposition to moralistic Christianity. However, in fighting legalism, these writers have often deviated into the opposite, and just as problematic, error of antinomianism. Though not promoting the *overt* antinomianism of John Agricola, these theologians put the law in an almost solely accusatory position and fail to emphasize the goodness and beauty of God's law as a guide for his creation.[29] Charles Arand and Joel Biermann summarize the situation well:

> Lutheranism in the twenty-first century finds itself in a unique situation. For the past five hundred years it has fought against conceiving of life only in terms of one kind of righteousness whereby human performance provided the basis for making the claim that God must accept us. But at times in the twentieth century, Lutheranism itself fell into its own form of one kind of righteousness whereby our passive righteousness before God became all we needed. And so active righteousness in conformity with the Law was left unstressed or was transformed into Gospel ways of talking.[30]

The primary error of the Roman Church, according to the Lutheran Confessions, is the neglect of teaching the two kinds of righteousness.[31] For the Lutheran reformers, righteousness can be spoken of in two distinct but important ways: First, and most importantly, there is passive righteousness. This is the sinner's justification, which is a result of the alien righteousness of Christ. This defines the sinner's life vertically, in his relationship with

28. Ibid., 60.

29. Agricola taught that the law should not, in any sense, be taught in church.

30. Arand, "Why the Two Kinds," 126.

31. This claim itself might be quite controversial, but its veracity will be demonstrated below.

God. On the other hand, there is active righteousness. This refers to the believer's sanctification, or incipient righteousness, whereby the believer is changed and lives a life of service to one's neighbor. This is how one lives in the world, before others. It is a horizontal reality. Rome made the mistake of speaking only of *one* kind of righteousness, namely, active righteousness. Similarly, much contemporary Lutheran theology has also emphasized only one kind of righteousness: passive righteousness. The distinction between these two kinds of righteousness helps provide the framework in which both antinomianism and legalism can be avoided. When Luther's distinction of the twofold righteousness is rightly expounded, the reductionistic leanings of contemporary Lutheran theology can be avoided, and pastors can be encouraged to proclaim the whole counsel of God, both law and gospel, justification and sanctification, within a traditionally Lutheran framework, without fear of compromising the free nature of the gospel.[32]

32. As Arand and Biermann observe: "Second, with reference to our human relationships, the two kinds of righteousness stress an active righteousness that gives Lutherans permission to speak positively about the Law within the Christian life without compromising or in any way threatening the doctrine of justification. It also expands our vision of Christian living in a way that includes all of our human activity in relationship to other human beings and the nonhuman creation" (Arand, "Why the Two Kinds," 128).

# Two Kinds of Righteousness

## Three Proposals

In the past sixty years, there has been a revival of Luther's teachings regarding vocation and the two kinds of righteousness. This has been especially prominent in the last two decades, primarily through the writings of several professors associated with Concordia Seminary in St. Louis, Missouri.[1] Numerous articles have been published on the subject within Lutheran theological journals, but the idea still remains in development. Because this is a relatively new (re)discovery in Lutheran theology, there are still several aspects to Luther's teaching of the two kinds of righteousness which have yet to be explored. In this chapter, three books will be discussed which have contributed to the ongoing theological dialogue regarding this important issue. First is Gustaf Wingren's *Luther on Vocation*, first published in 1958 and translated into English in 1961, which brought the doctrine of vocation back into theological discourse. Second is *The Genius of Luther's Theology*, which is the first lengthy treatment of the two kinds of righteousness in a systematic fashion, written by Charles Arand and Robert Kolb. The third book to be examined is *A Case for Character*, by Joel Biermann, which presents a case for three kinds of righteousness. In examining these three texts, the development of this theme will be explored within these various writers, and the positive and negative aspects of each approach will be explained in view of the continued development of this theme.

---

1. The phrase "St. Louis theology" has sometimes been thrown around in popular parlance to refer to this teaching on the twofold righteousness.

## Luther on Vocation

The contemporary revival of Luther's doctrine of the two kinds of righteousness began with a renewed study of the concept of vocation in Luther's thought. Gustaf Wingren's *Luther on Vocation* remains the classic text on this subject, wherein he argues that Luther frames the Christian life primarily in terms of vocation before the world. Though this book is not explicitly a treatise on the two kinds of righteousness, this distinction is the grounding behind most of Wingren's argument.

When Wingren speaks of the *vocatio*, he is not referring to its common scholastic meaning, which is tied specially to the call by which one is made a Christian, nor is he referring to the pastoral call. Rather, he is speaking of various earthly vocations to which one is called. Essentially, a "vocation is a 'station' which is by nature helpful to others if it be followed."[2] This does not necessarily mean one's occupation, but also refers to one's place in the family and community. One then has multiple vocations in his life. One could, for example, be a father, brother, son, baker, congregant, and husband. These are all different stations into which the individual has been placed.

For Wingren, vocation is always a station in which one has opportunity to serve the neighbor. Christian morality is essentially defined by the love shown in different stations of one's life.[3] This love and service is not an autonomous set of actions, but God himself works through the believer in his vocations. Wingren notes that even in the act of milking cows, God is at work.[4] This is an aspect of the *creatio continua* which characterizes Wingren's corpus of work.[5] God continues his work of creation, through preservation, as he serves the world through the hands of others. This is because vocation is not concerned with heaven, but is instead concerned with this world—the world of creation. Wingren argues that God carries out the continuance of his work of creation when one "bends oneself down toward the world."[6] The downward focus of God himself in both creation and redemption is reflected in his creation, as renewed people are also focused

---

2. Wingren, *Luther on Vocation*, 4.

3. Ibid., 6.

4. Ibid., 9.

5. Wingren's idea of creation is extensively explained in his book Creation and Law.

6. Wingren, *Luther on Vocation*, 10.

downward. For Wingren, this creational emphasis defines the nature of the Christian's active righteousness in the world and *for* the world.

There is an important distinction between one's relationship to heaven, which is established solely by faith, and one's relationship to fellow human creatures based on love. Wingren explains:

> In heaven, before God, vocation has as little to contribute as do good works. Good works and vocation (love) exist for the earth and one's neighbor, not for eternity and God. God does not need our good works, but our neighbor does. It is faith that God wants. Faith ascends to heaven. Faith enters a different kingdom, the eternal, divine kingdom, which Luther considers just as evident as the earthly realm, with its offices and occupations through which God carries on his creative work. In the heavenly kingdom Christ is king and there the gospel alone rules: no law, and therefore no works.[7]

Wingren purports an absolute divide between earth and heaven. They both require different things from the believer: earth requires works, and heaven requires faith. These two kinds of righteousness are both essential, but must not be mixed. He states strongly that from vocation is irrelevant from the vertical standpoint of faith.[8] Wingren further urges that the two distinctive realms of heaven and earth, through which faith and love operate, must be kept distinct, as essential as both of these realities are.[9] In this manner, Wingren anticipates later writings on the subject of the two kinds of righteousness.

Relationships between fellow humans and before God are set in contradistinction to one another. Before God, no other individuals matter other than the one who stands before God, either in faith or unbelief.[10] One's status and stations in life are completely irrelevant before the throne of God. The only differentiating factor between persons in heaven and those who are not is the reality of faith. In heaven the standing of all persons is identical. All stand in the grace of God. Here, the gospel alone rules, and there is no distinction in the realm of law.[11] Faith "must rise up to God himself

---

7. Ibid., 10.
8. Ibid., 11.
9. Ibid., 12.
10. Ibid., 13.
11. Ibid., 13.

and rest in him; faith is entrance into heaven."[12] Faith is an eschatological reality, as it places us into God's heavenly kingdom, bringing us above the earthly kingdom which exists here and now to the kingdom of God. This particular eschatological emphasis of justification is a unique factor in Wingren's thought, as opposed to some other Lutheran theologians. In descriptions of the nature of passive righteousness (justification), Lutheran scholastics sometimes focus so much on the temporal *ordo salutis* that this eschatological dimension of Luther's thought is neglected.

In the earthly realm, Wingren argues, the human creature cooperates with God in preserving the world. There is strong distinction between two spheres: "above us," and "below us." There is no cooperation in the divine-human relationship, but there is in the human-human relationship in the world below. In cooperating with God's work by serving the neighbor, man becomes a "mask of God" to the world. Through man, God serves this earth, though his work remains unrecognized, because it appears to be solely the work of human hands. The love which the creature has comes from God, and flows "down to human beings on earth through all vocations, through both spiritual and earthly governments."[13] This work must happen, because God's eschatological word of imputation is not yet realized. Instead, deeds play a large role in one's status in the world. The Christian's vocation then is an aspect of the now-and-not-yet reality of Christian existence prior to the consummation of God's kingdom.

Wingren expounds upon the role of cooperation between the creature and the Creator by way of analogy. He speaks of an earthly slave and his master. In this type of relationship, the serf is in some sense "free," in that he can choose how to move his body, what to say, and so forth. However, he is still in bondage to his master, so that he must live under and with the rule of his owner. Wingren writes, "When the slave, using all the strength and understanding he has, does what he is commanded in field and meadow, he is his master's 'fellow-worker.'"[14] The cooperation of the human creature is limited to the earthly realm. It is directed to fellow human beings rather than God.[15] At times, Wingren speaks specifically about the Christian as one who cooperates with God. He notes that God works together with man

12. Ibid., 20.
13. Ibid., 28.
14. Ibid., 124.
15. Ibid., 124.

when "a Christian directs his service downward to others."[16] Other times, however, Wingren confesses that unregenerate people can in some sense even cooperate with God, though unknowingly.[17] Wingren is able to say this because he places the distinction between the two kinds of righteousness within the context of the two kingdoms. If cooperation belongs to the realm "below us," and that realm contains both regenerate and unregenerate persons, cooperation must necessarily belong to both the believer and the unbeliever.[18] Here is a place where Wingren's distinction fails to take into account the difference between the believer and unbeliever in relation to good works. According to the Formula of Concord, cooperation, or synergy, with God is a unique reality of the regenerate Christian, whose will has been liberated by the grace of God (FC SD II.63).

Wingren seeks to answer the question regarding the difference between the active righteousness and cooperation of the unbeliever and the believer by arguing that, with the unbeliever, God works without his Holy Spirit.[19] The difference then between the righteous pagan and the righteous Christian is in terms of the possession of the third person of the Holy Trinity. This distinction deserves further development, as divine indwelling lays the groundwork for emphasizing the *unio mystica* as the primary differentiating factor between the Christian and the non-Christian. The Christian, being regenerated, has a special relationship to God and is thus opened up in a new way for service unto the neighbor. Wingren then cites Luther, who mentions three specific things which pertain to the active cooperative righteousness of the Christian: "the putting to death of the flesh, love to others, and humility before God."[20] Interestingly, two of these three aspects of the Christian life mentioned by Luther are not simply horizontally focused, but also reference one's relationship to God. Yet, even after explaining these important distinctions between the obedience of the believer and the unbeliever, Wingren argues that the motivation of the Christian and the purity of one's heart are irrelevant to faith. The only aspect of one's deeds which matters is its effect upon the neighbor.[21] This is where Wingren's above-us/

16. Ibid., 126.

17. Ibid., 131.

18. "Thus we see the role of co-operation in relation to the two kingdoms: co-operation is barred from heaven, and relevant to earth" (ibid., 128).

19. Ibid., 131.

20. Ibid.

21. Ibid., 133.

below-us dichotomy shows its weakness. In heaven, before God, all that matters is faith, and not good works in any way, whether that is their external benefit to others or the purity of motivation in performing them. On earth, what matters is the final result achieved for the sake of the neighbor, and motivation is irrelevant. There is simply no place for a right motivation and will to have any particular benefit either in heaven or on earth. This is problematic in light of a number of biblical texts which state otherwise.

There is an eschatological tension in which the believer lives. By love, he serves his present situation, as he exists in the "now" of the present age. However, the believer also lives in the "not yet" of God's coming kingdom. Wingren argues that works have only the present existence in view, but faith has eschatological focus.[22] According to one's old man, the aspect of oneself which is not yet renewed, one asks about the "righteousness of his works."[23] However, faith and "the new man only knows one righteousness: the forgiveness of sins."[24] It is this righteousness, rather than the righteousness of works (i.e., civil righteousness) which drives one to seek the good of the neighbor, because the Christian looks not to heaven, but to his neighbor who needs the performance of good deeds.[25] This contention continues to demonstrate that Wingren has no place in his theological system for heavenly rewards for good deeds performed in faith.

The earthly realm is also one of intense suffering. Wingren notes that the "Christian is crucified by the law in his vocation, under the earthly government."[26] The earthly kingdom serves as law, pointing one to the heavenly kingdom—the gospel. Through vocation, the believer must bear his cross, just as Christ bore his. In one's various stations, the believer works his various duties out of the overflow of love in his heart, but is met with ingratitude and rejection, as was Christ himself.[27] Works of service must be done, not out of compulsion or hope of reward, but out of love for the neighbor.

The nature of sinful humanity confuses faith with love. Because of his sinful nature, man "exalts himself above others" because of his works,

22. Ibid., 37–38.
23. Ibid., 45.
24. Ibid.
25. Ibid.
26. Ibid., 30.
27. Ibid., 31.

instead of with faith.[28] The human person thus rejects his need for divine pardon, viewing his own good deeds as meritorious as he conflates these two divergent kingdoms.[29] Regeneration reorients man, so that he now understands the proper place of his good works. He realizes that his relationship to God is a purely passive one, whereby he is to stand before God purely in faith. Because of this, he is now able to freely perform good works in their proper sphere: for the neighbor.

Wingren explicitly expounds upon the two kinds of righteousness by distinguishing between the *iustitia civilis* (civil righteousness) and *iustitia christiana* (righteousness of Christ).[30] He defines these two kinds of righteousness in this way: "Civil righteousness is promoted by the law and is relevant in courts, in general, before man, as an adequate righteousness. Righteousness in Christ is a given righteousness, and can be said to consist of the forgiveness of sins."[31] This active, or civil, righteousness is at work primarily in one's vocation, whereas the primary focus of the church is upward, to the kingdom of glory.[32] Wingren explains these two kinds of righteousness in terms of the two kinds of relationships that each person has. He notes that through each type of righteousness, man is put into right relationship to each of God's realms. In passive righteousness, by faith, one is rightly related to God. In active righteousness, by love, one is rightly related to the earth.[33] By faith, one is incorporated into Christ, and by love one is incorporated into the life of the world. This exposition serves as the groundwork upon which all later proponents of the two kinds of righteousness build, as Wingren connects the two types of righteousness to two sets of relationships: divine and human.

Though distinguished, these two kinds of righteousness have an intimate connection. Wingren argues that these two essential aspects of the regenerate person are never to be divorced.[34] Faith is not a decision of the human will for Wingren, but it is Christ himself. Because of the identity of Christ and faith, the believer must necessarily perform good works, because it is Christ performing good works for the neighbor through the one

28. Ibid., 61.
29. Ibid.
30. Ibid., 20.
31. Ibid.
32. Ibid., 28.
33. Ibid., 33.
34. Ibid., 32.

who believes. The good works which are performed are spontaneous and unexpected, because in the one who has believed the gospel, a love arises for the neighbor, which is a surprising reality.[35] The good works performed in service of others are not coerced, nor are they something that the believer tries hard at. Instead, they come naturally. Wingren explains:

> There is nothing more delightful and lovable on earth than one's neighbor. Love does not think about doing works, it finds joy in people; and when something good is done for others, that does not appear to love as works but simply as gifts which flow naturally from love. Love never does something because it has to. It is permitted to act. And earth "with its trees and grass" is the site of man's vocation. He who has the Holy Spirit knows it by the fact, among others, that in faith and gladness he fulfils his vocation. He rejoices in his labor.[36]

Wingren attempts to see the relationship between faith and works within the regenerate person. One's faith is identified with Christ himself, and thus one must spontaneously do good simply for the sake of the other person. This is not something one *tries* to do, but something God does through him as a mask. While Wingren helpfully explains the free nature of the Spirit's work within the Christian, his emphasis on the spontaneity of good works might leave the reader with the impression that one must not expend effort in sanctification. This is opposed to Article II of the Formula of Concord.

The question of personal piety naturally arises in view of Wingren's "active before the world, and passive before God" distinction which he utilizes throughout the work. It would seem that the life of prayer, fasting, and other such spiritual disciplines relate not to one's horizontal relationship, but instead to the vertical relationship one has with God. If this is the case, then it would seem to negate the passivity in that relationship. Wingren attempts to solve that dilemma by arguing that for the Christian, "Prayer and faith become identical."[37] Faith is not an active work on earth, but rather, it is the opening up of oneself to God as a passive recipient of his gifts. Wingren places prayer in the realm of the law's second use. It is an act of humility and a request for mercy, under the condemning word of law. Yet prayer also has a horizontal focus, in that prayers are answered in and through the vocations of others, and in that it is the trials in one's vocation

35. Ibid., 41.
36. Ibid., 43–44.
37. Ibid., 187.

which lead to prayer. While Wingren is correct in emphasizing the passive nature of prayer, as well as the connection between vocation and the need for and answers to prayer, this solution still fails to capture the multifaceted nature of Christian piety as expressed in holy Scripture and the Lutheran tradition. The primary issue is the nature of prayers of thanksgiving offered in response to passive righteousness. Though God does not *need* prayers of thanksgiving in the sense that the neighbor needs prayer, the believer is in some sense active in praying or singing words of thanksgiving. It is this vertical necessity of eucharistic sacrifice which is absent in Wingren, as well as in other proponents of the two kinds of righteousness. This category of eucharistic sacrifice solves a number of problems with a pure horizontal understanding of God's law. If love toward God and upward piety are placed solely in the category of thanksgiving, then love toward God is always in response to passive righteousness. Thereby, the passivity of the divine-human relationship is affirmed without neglecting the first table of divine law. This, then, affirms Wingren's central convictions about the divine-human relationship, while simultaneously giving account of all the biblical data.

The concept of love is the missing piece in older Luther research, according to Wingren. The emphasis on divine pardon within Luther's thought has caused some scholars to neglect the human-human relationship based on love within Luther's theology.[38] This has resulted in a truncated view of the Christian life, to the neglect of Christian sanctification. This contention is the primary benefit of Wingren's work in the broad world of Luther scholarship. Instead of focusing solely on the doctrine of justification, Wingren expounds upon Luther's theology of the Christian life. Because of this work, the doctrine of vocation has been treated extensively in popular Lutheran discourse, strengthening the preaching of pastors as well as the layman's understanding of his place within God's creation. The above-us/below-us dichotomy allows Wingren to speak about the importance of both justification and sanctification without compromising the centrality of justification as the final word of God in the divine-human relationship.

While his book is an essential piece of scholarship because it brought about the contemporary discourse concerning the Christian's relationship to the world, the gospel, and the law, there are several areas where Wingren's ideas are inadequate for a comprehensive discussion of the two kinds of righteousness in Christian theology. First, Wingren limits discussion about Christian life to that of vocation, which, while quite an extensive

---

38. Ibid., 54.

category, does not completely encapsulate Luther's meaning of active righteousness. Though Wingren does discuss prayer, there is an insufficient focus on the first table of the law and of the relationship between the two tables. This is where a discussion of the nature of thanksgiving would aid and strengthen his argument. Wingren also limits the law to two uses in Luther's theology, which does not comport with the Large Catechism or the historic Lutheran tradition. Consequently, Wingren has an inadequate basis on which to discuss practical ethics in the Christian life. He also does not sufficiently explain the difference between civil and inchoate righteousness in the horizontal realm. As beneficial as it is in constructing a doctrine of sanctification, the strict above-us/below-us dichotomy utilized by Wingren does not explain two prominent New Testament teachings: the rewards for horizontal good works in heaven, and the role of motivation in performing good deeds. For this reason, the good deeds of the Christian and the heathen become almost indistinguishable. These problems are solved by adding the third category of *thanksgiving* as a vertical reality in the Christian's life of faith. This does not compromise the free nature of the divine-human relationship, because thanksgiving is always offered *in response* to the reception of vertical righteousness. Wingren also overstates the free nature of good works in the horizontal realm. One might get the impression, through this work, that one should exercise no conscious effort in Christian sanctification since good deeds flow spontaneously from faith. As will be discussed below, Joel Biermann corrects this problem through the use of virtue ethics. Finally, as is the case in most treatments of the two kinds of righteousness, any notion of the *unio mystica*, which is essential to both Luther and the Formula of Concord, is missing. Though some shortcomings remain, Wingren's work is still one of the most essential works of Luther research in the twentieth century, and is an indispensable book in any discourse regarding the Lutheran approach to the Christian's existence in the world.

## The Genius of Luther's Theology

Robert Kolb and Charles Arand, professors of theology at Concordia Seminary in St. Louis, wrote the first book-length treatment of Luther's theology of the two kinds of righteousness and its relevance to Christian theology. In *The Genius of Luther's Theology*, Kolb and Arand present Luther's theology through the lens of the distinction between the two kinds of righteousness as a thoroughgoing theological paradigm. They draw heavily on Wingren's earth-heaven distinction, while adding a number of distinct elements to the two-kinds-of-righteousness paradigm.

Relationship is an essential anthropological question. Christian theological textbooks have most often discussed the nature of the *imago Dei* and original sin under "the doctrine of man" while neglecting other aspects of the human person. Kolb and Arand seek to remedy this problem by proposing that Luther's distinction between the two kinds of righteousness explains the place of the human creature within the two essential human relationships: one's relation to God and one's relation to fellow human persons. This teaching is described as a "nervous system" which runs throughout the entire corpus of Christian doctrine, and as an essential element of the Lutheran Reformation.[39] The believer is related to God due to passive righteousness, by which God grants the righteousness of Christ through his re-creative word.[40] The human creature is related to other people by means of active righteousness—living in one's station in life while serving the neighbor. It is the "passive righteousness of faith" which "provides the core identity of a person." Active righteousness "flows from that core identity out into the world."[41] This is an expansion on Wingren's connection between righteousness and relationship. For Wingren, one is related to God by faith and to the neighbor by love. Kolb and Arand argue that these two relationships are essential to the human person's identity.

Both kinds of righteousness are necessary to be "completely human."[42] These kinds of righteousness are not opposed to one another, nor should they be conflated with each other. Kolb and Arand argue that passive righteousness serves as the ground of active righteousness. They argue that there is an intimate connection between the twofold types of righteousness. The passive righteousness of faith descends to earth, and then flows forth from the believer into the world.[43] This connection between justification and sanctification helps to connect these two realities of faith and love, which at times in Wingren's writings sound almost as if they have no inherent and internal connection to one another.[44] Holding onto these two kinds

39. Kolb and Arand, *Genius of Luther's Theology*, 25.

40. Ibid., 26.

41. Ibid.

42. Ibid., 29.

43. Ibid., 30.

44. Though, as noted above, he sees the connection in the person of Christ who he

of righteousness correctly is difficult for humans to do, because people are naturally inclined to believe in only one kind of righteousness. Holding only to the righteousness of faith allows one to fall into antinomianism, whereas focusing only on active righteousness confuses one's relationship with God with that of the neighbor, becoming legalism. Kolb and Arand, like Wingren, seek to emphasize the realities of both faith and love in Lutheran theology and practice.

Kolb and Arand explain passive righteousness in a discussion of the nature of human identity. They argue that faith is at "the core of human existence," because to be fully human is to passively receive God's gifts.[45] Before God, one finds identity as a creature, in opposition to Creator. This involves a confession of oneself as a recipient of gifts rather than an active participant in that relationship.[46] Faith is not accidental to human existence, but is at the very heart of one's being. We gain this understanding in faith, wherein the believer receives the alien righteousness of Christ. This alien righteousness is not simply the righteousness of God's essential divine nature, but it is identified with Christ's substitutionary life as a second Adam, along with his vicarious death.[47] This theme of identity is not present in Wingren, but it is an extrapolation of the theme of these two kinds of righteousness beyond where it is utilized in earlier treatments, including that of Luther himself.

Human creatures are not simply passive in the application of salvation, but also in the act of creation itself. Kolb and Arand expound upon the nature of God's word, writing: "God's Word says what it does and does what it says."[48] This is exactly what the creation consists of. God spoke, and through his word all things were created. In the same manner, God's declarative word of righteousness makes one righteous. Utilizing the work of Oswald Bayer, Kolb and Arand are heavily indebted to contemporary

---

identifies with faith. This connection, however, is not always apparent in his writing.

45. Kolb and Arand, *Genius of Luther's Theology*, 38.

46. Ibid.

47. In this context, Kolb argues, "Here one must be careful about dogmatizing atonement theories, for this satisfaction was no buyout or payoff. It was execution. The law collected wages of sin by condemning and executing him. The cross is where God carried out his judgment" (ibid., 40). Kolb seems to be conflating the traditional definition of the vicarious atonement in the Anselmian tradition with a bizarre caricature taken from Gerhard Forde. He is not being consistent with the nature of the atonement in traditional Lutheran scholastic theology.

48. Ibid., 42.

speech-act theory as a valid methodology to explain Luther's doctrine of justification. God's creative word stands at the beginning of the cosmos and encapsulates the entire life of faith. Creation, preservation, and salvation are all dependent upon the divine speech-act.

Within the context of the effective word, Kolb and Arand seek to explain the relationship between passive righteousness (justification) and active righteousness (sanctification):

> There is no debate between "forensic" righteousness and "essen-tial" righteousness. To put it this way, as Gerhard Forde remarked, is to pose false alternatives. He argues that "the absolutely forensic character of justification renders it effective—justification that actually kills and makes alive. It is to be sure, 'not only' forensic, but that is the case only because the more forensic it is, the more effective it is!" Thus, justification is not a legal fiction. The word does what it says. When God declares a person to be righteous, that person is actually righteous. The Word has brought about a new reality. A new relationship has been established.[49]

Actual inherent righteousness is a result of passive righteousness. The effective word changes the heart, and is thus the cause of good works within the believer. In this context, Kolb and Arand argue against any notion of theosis within Lutheran thought as contradictory with Luther's word-centric metaphysic. They argue that salvation is not, in any sense, an ontological change. Rather than Greek substance ontology, Luther is committed to a holistic and relational conception of human identity.[50] In view of this relational approach to the human person, Kolb and Arand argue that *simul iustus et peccator* refers only to total states, and not to partial realities. Thus active righteousness, for Arand and Kolb, cannot be within the category of the believer's becoming more righteous, or becoming more like God ontologically. This is the primary problem in Kolb and Arand's treatment of the two kinds of righteousness. While they rightly emphasize the importance of this distinction in Luther's thought, and the manner in which it explains the various relationships which humans have, there is essentially no place for either progressive sanctification or the mystical union. In this sense, they do not significantly depart from the theology of Gerhard Forde or other proponents of Radical Lutheranism, though they do confess the

49. Ibid., 43.
50. Ibid., 49.

validity of the law's third use within the Christian's life. These problems will be addressed below.

There is a robust theology of creation in Kolb and Arand's work, as taken from Wingren. They argue that Luther spoke not primarily of the initial act of creation when treating the First Article of the Creed, but of the *creatio continua*. Mankind was given dominion over creation and is called to accept his place as a part of the created order rather than trying to rise above it. Kolb and Arand utilize Wingren's emphasis on the *larvae Dei* (masks of God). Human beings "are the instruments by which [God] provides and preserves life."[51] Through their various vocations, God causes the world to function. The reality of sin in the world has not stopped God's continual creation and preservation.[52] This is true of both believers and unbelievers, as God guides the actions of all human persons for the purpose of divine preservation.[53] In this way, human creatures become co-workers with God, carrying out his will in granting general welfare to the creation. In all of these areas, Kolb and Arand affirm synergism in the human person's relationship to the world.

Sanctification, for Kolb and Arand, is an essential aspect of Christian theology. They posit that the emphasis on justification by faith does not negate the reality and importance of good works for the Christian. They note that the reception of passive righteousness does not annul the importance of good works *coram mundo*.[54] Rather, passive righteousness causes the Christian to be active in society. However, there is no "sharp line of distinction" between the righteous works of the believer and the unbeliever.[55] The difference between the active righteousness of the unbeliever and that of the Christian is that believers do not live in an attempt at self-justification, but in view of God's life-giving verdict.[56] Faith causes one to cease living purely for the self, and instead to look outward, to the needs of others. God's justifying word causes one to return to one's created responsibilities. Kolb and Arand note that "the Lutheran doctrine of justification expresses itself in a robust doctrine of vocation that the Christian embraces as one

51. Ibid., 55.
52. Ibid., 56.
53. Ibid., 57.
54. Ibid., 103.
55. Ibid.
56. Ibid.

reenters creation."[57] Good works in one's vocation are a necessary result of passive righteousness.

The two kinds of righteousness allow one to live both in the heavenly realm before God, and in the creaturely realm before other human beings. Within the world, "faith embraces the most menial activities,"[58] such as changing an infant's diaper, as in accord with God's good will. This extends especially to the family. Marriage is not a "straightjacket that keeps [husband and wife] from seeking multiple lovers," but it is a good gift of God, and a station in life through which one might serve.[59] Parents should view their children's roles in a similar manner, and children should also view their parents likewise. The needs which must be attended to in these various stations are not purely physical, but through them one has an opportunity to obey Christ's commission to share the gospel with others.[60] In all of these ways, Christians are able to delight in and begin to obey the law by living in the created realm.

Kolb and Arand speak about sanctification as a work of the Holy Spirit. In some sense, sanctification is a perfect reality, but in another sense, it is a work in progress. They argue that the righteousness of faith is a complete righteousness, but the Christian's works constitute a partial righteousness.[61] In seeking to maintain their previous contention that the *simul* is only about total states, Kolb and Arand argue that the righteousness of Christ is perfect, but appears to be partial in view of the world. They assert that many views of progressive sanctification would negate the need for God's continual imputation, or that somehow God's righteousness would be replaced by man's. Luther, in this view, rejects every notion of "Aristotle's model of increasing holiness,"[62] even within the realm of active righteousness. Kolb and Arand state that "sanctification is not a process whereby we move from 57 percent holy to 58 percent holy. The Christian is 100 percent holy and now tries to manifest that righteousness, to make it known in daily life, in spite of the resistance to sin."[63] Good works are the result of complete and perfect righteousness, which is eschatological righteousness manifested

---

57. Ibid., 107.
58. Ibid., 112.
59. Ibid., 113.
60. Ibid.
61. Ibid., 124.
62. Ibid., 125.
63. Ibid., 126.

now. Kolb and Arand expand upon Wingren's utilization of eschatology in relation to passive righteousness, but do so in such a way as to negate the traditional Lutheran teaching about sanctification as a progressive reality.

Kolb and Arand's work is helpful in that it applies Luther's insight regarding the two kinds of righteousness to various areas of life and theology. They helpfully explain the role of the Christian in the created realm, and the importance of passive righteousness as the central reality from which good works flow. However, there are some problems within Kolb and Arand's proposal. First, they do not give an extensive differentiation between the believer's good works and those of the non-Christian. Though they emphasize the reality of faith, there is no attention given to the reality of regeneration and the indwelling of Christ within the believer. Second, the manner in which the *simul* is explained does not allow for progress in sanctification in any real sense, which is essential to Luther's understanding of the active righteousness of the Christian. Finally, though Kolb and Arand are correct in their aversion to certain forms of deification, they leave no place for historic Lutheran teaching of the *unio mystica*, which is an important part of Luther's teaching regarding the two kinds of righteousness. While this work does have its flaws, it is a helpful look at the importance of the two-kinds-of-righteousness theme in view of the different kinds of human relationships and vocations.

## A Case for Character: Towards a Lutheran Virtue Ethics

Joel Biermann, Professor of Systematic Theology at Concordia Seminary in St. Louis, Missouri, has written a defense of the distinction between the two kinds of righteousness in his book *A Case for Character: Towards a Lutheran Virtue Ethics*. In this work, Biermann argues against a law-gospel reductionist paradigm, wherein the third use of the law is either denied or neglected in theology and pastoral practice. In contradistinction to this problem in contemporary Lutheran discourse, he contends that the two kinds of righteousness helps to clarify the role of good works and the law in the life of the Christian in a way in which the simple law-gospel paradigm cannot. Biermann expounds upon several missing aspects of Wingren's and Kolb and Arand's two-kinds-of-righteousness proposals.

The pastoral implications of the two kinds of righteousness are at the heart of Biermann's work. He opens it with a story about a pastor who is going to preach on Colossians 3:18–25. This text explains the necessity of particular behaviors in one's relationships with other human creatures. Working from a law-gospel-only paradigm, the preacher cannot preach about explicit moral behaviors called for in this text. Therefore, he uses this text to demonstrate that such holy living is impossible in the lives of his people, and that therefore Christ's righteousness covers the inherent weakness of the human creature to carry out these duties. The problem here is that one is simply not taking the text for what it says, because the law-gospel-reductionist approach has no place for concrete moral instruction.

In contrast to this prevailing notion, Biermann argues that it is part of the purpose and function of the church to inculcate virtue and morality in the lives of its people. It is part of the church's call to develop the Christian character of its members.[64] Biermann does not intend to supplant the Lutheran church's clear gospel proclamation with something else, as if to replace the Lutheran emphasis on justification. He contends strongly that "Justification by grace through faith in Jesus Christ alone remains the church's central doctrine and *raison d'etre*."[65] That does not mean, however, that the church is limited in its role of proclamation simply to this single message. Alongside of its gospel emphasis, the church must also inculcate moral living. Biermann proposes that the church should do this by way of ethical formation within the context of Luther's doctrine of the two kinds of righteousness. Though utilizing the same distinction, Biermann's intent in writing this work is different than those of Wingren, Kolb, and Arand. Wingren utilizes this distinction to emphasize the importance and reality of love toward the neighbor in the Christian life. Kolb and Arand explicate its importance for Christian anthropology. Biermann, in contrast, utilizes this distinction with a view to inculcate Christian ethics in catechesis and preaching.

In the latter chapters of his book, which are the most significant to our current project, Biermann offers a proposal which seeks to establish the importance of ethical formation in a confessionally Lutheran framework. He contends, "What is needed is a framework that can account for the wide range of material found in the Lutheran Confessions that is at once doctrinal and ethical."[66] Biermann is highly critical of emphasizing "motivation" in ethical discussions, which has been a consistent theme in Lutheran ethical work. He explains, "The frame follows a logical or theo-

---

64. Biermann, *Case for Character*, 6.

65. Ibid., 6.

66. Ibid., 107.

logical progression like this: God grants salvation purely by divine grace, and so overcome with the resultant gratitude is the redeemed person that the life of sanctification inevitably blossoms."[67] In this perspective, any extensive exhortation in preaching is essentially meaningless, because it is the gospel alone which effects a life of obedience, with no role for the law in the life of the believer. These good works are purely spontaneous, and thus should not be discussed, lest one be motivated by the law rather than the gospel. This is the danger of an overemphasis on the spontaneity of good works as is found in Wingren's writing. Biermann notes that this approach to sanctification is problematic, as is apparent not only through theological argumentation, but by observation of reality.[68] It is demonstrably not always the case that pure gospel proclamation, without exhortation, results in continued growth in obedience. Ultimately, Biermann contends that motivation cannot be utilized as a framework for ethics from a confessional or scriptural perspective.[69] This makes ethical discussion a psychological and introspective practice, wherein one is constantly looking inward in examination of one's motives and desires. Instead, one should focus on ethical actions themselves.

The second framework examined by Biermann is law and gospel. He argues that the distinction between law and gospel has sometimes become a polarity between the two words of God. When this happens, the third use of the law is neglected. Biermann argues that the "unintended fruit of a law/gospel framework may be either a legalistic self-absorption in self-justifying works (the loss of the gospel), or at the opposite extreme, the very licentious and antinomian attitudes that prompted this study (the loss of the law)."[70] The ethical proposals of Carter Lindberg and Gerhard Forde are rejected by Biermann as inadequate. While law and gospel serve as the perfect framework regarding one's *coram Deo* relationship, it is an insufficient framework for answering ethical questions. He concludes that law and gospel "used as an overall framework . . . is finally detrimental to the vitality of Lutheranism," due to its inadequacy to deal with every theological and ethical concern.[71] Like Kolb and Arand, Biermann argues that another theological paradigm must stand next to law and gospel in order

67. Ibid., 108.
68. Ibid., 110.
69. Ibid., 114.
70. Ibid., 116.
71. Ibid., 118.

to explicate aspects of the Christian faith which the law-gospel framework was not formulated to address.

After demonstrating the weaknesses of both motivation and law and gospel as frameworks in which to place Christian ethics, Biermann gives an overview of the two-kinds-of-righteousness framework proposed by Kolb and Arand. He argues that this has provided a "much more effective framework within which to consider the complexities of faith and life than does the law-and-gospel dialectic just considered."[72] Unlike law and gospel, the two-kinds-of-righteousness framework allows for one to consider concrete questions regarding ethics *coram mundo*, rather than limiting ethical discourse to the *coram Deo* relationship. There is, however, still some ambiguity in utilizing this language. While Luther's definition of active righteousness is focused on the righteousness of the Christian who has faith, in view of the reality of divine imputation, Melanchthon uses the phrase "active righteousness" to refer to civil righteousness, of both believers and the unregenerate. Because of the inconsistency in identifying the two kinds of righteousness, the two-kinds-of-righteousness paradigm falls short of being a comprehensive ethical framework.

In light of the shortcomings of the previous three paradigms for ethics, Biermann proposes that instead of two kinds of righteousness, Lutheran theologians would do well to adopt a teaching of three kinds of righteousness. This proposal allows for both Luther's and Melanchthon's definitions of active righteousness. There is passive righteousness (justification), active righteousness (sanctification), and civil righteousness (the righteousness that benefits society regardless of faith). This distinction arises from Luther's 1518 sermon titled "On Threefold Righteousness." Biermann argues that this distinction between three kinds of righteousness is consistent in the writings of Luther and Melanchthon. He contends that both reformers do not only distinguish between vertical and horizontal righteousness, but they also argue for an extensive differentiation between the active righteousness of the Christian and that of the pagan.[73] Biermann defines these three separate kinds of righteousness:

> This first kind of righteousness is roughly parallel to what Luther called apparent righteousness, and what Melanchthon labeled righteousness of reason. The second righteousness is the righteousness of salvation that comes from outside, through faith.

72. Ibid.
73. Ibid., 125.

What is being called here the second kind of righteousness, Luther named, among a variety of other terms, alien righteousness. Melanchthon termed it the righteousness of promise and considered it third. The third kind of righteousness in this threefold framework is the righteousness that is evident in the godly lives and good works of Christians as they function within the created world.[74]

Each of these three kinds of righteousness is good and important for the proper functioning of God's creation, but each must play its proper role so that they are not conflated with one another.

Biermann argues that these three kinds of righteousness, though remaining distinct, are intimately connected to one another. He notes that the first (civic) and third (inchoate) kinds of righteousness share several similarities. They are both centered on the relationships that one has horizontally.[75] These types of righteousness are both *coram mundo* realities, concerned with performing God's will within creation. The difference remains, however, in the faith and motivation of the one performing these deeds. Biermann explains they differ in three ways: first, the motivation differs. Second, the goal for which one works differs; the unregenerate person performs active righteousness for the sake of self-justification, whereas the Christian does so freely. Finally, the Holy Spirit works in a unique manner in the life of the regenerate person.[76] Biermann improves upon an argument of Wingren, who occasionally mentions that some distinction must be made between the horizontal work of the Christian and that of the unbeliever, without giving an extensive account of this difference. Unfortunately, Biermann's comments on this matter are very brief, and while the solution he poses is correct, it would greatly benefit the dialogue surrounding the three kinds of righteousness for this distinction to be expounded.

The connection between the second and third kind of righteousness is also explored by Biermann. These two types of righteousness come in contact with one another in a chart Biermann draws relating these three kinds of righteousness, illustrated by three lines. There are two horizontal lines, representing governing and conforming righteousness, and one vertical line, symbolizing justifying righteousness, which intersects with conforming righteousness but not governing righteousness. Passive righteousness serves somehow as a basis for the Christian's active life in the world,

74. Ibid., 127.
75. Ibid., 129.
76. Ibid., 130.

whereas it does not do so in relation to the unbeliever's civic righteousness. These two kinds of righteousness are connected in that "They are both, in a sense, the righteousness of Christians: the second or justifying righteousness is the righteousness that is passively received; the third or conforming righteousness is the righteousness that is actively lived."[77] Biermann argues that while theologians have often attempted to explain the nature of the connection between passive and active righteousness, one should simply accept that they are united without further explanation.[78] The new obedience of the Christian in sanctification and justification are somehow related, but that relation is not explored because it is not explained in either the Confessions or in Scripture.[79] In contrast to this, Kolb and Arand argue that the connection is found in God's speech-act, and Wingren views the connection as Christ himself who is identified with faith.

According to Biermann, there is a connection between these three kinds of righteousness, the three uses of the law, and the three articles of the Creed. The firsts of each of these distinct theological categories are about creation: civil righteousness, the civil use of the law, and the Father as Creator. The second are about redemption: passive righteousness, the pedagogical use of the law, and Christ as Redeemer. The third items are about the application of redemption through the Holy Spirit: incipient Christian righteousness, the didactic use of the law, and the sanctification of the Holy Spirit. In this manner, the three-kinds-of-righteousness model is in accord with both the catholic tradition and the Lutheran Confessions. Biermann is not proposing a theological novelty.

The doctrine of creation is especially important in Biermann's proposal. Utilizing Wingren, Biermann argues that all three kinds of righteousness function within the realm of creation. Redemption itself is creational, as God utilized a human nature in the incarnation to accomplish redemption. This redemption is applied, similarly, by means of the created order, through word and sacrament. Creation is not something which the believer needs to escape from, but the Spirit works to "restore it to God's original creative intent."[80] The Christian's good works also function within the created realm because "God does not redeem people from creation,

77. Ibid.

78. Ibid., 131.

79. Biermann thus rejects the argument of Arand and Kolb that the relationship between justification and sanctification lies in the nature of the effective speech-act.

80. Biermann, *Case for Character*, 151.

but for creation."[81] Biermann argues for a "creedal framework" for his three-kinds-of-righteousness proposal, because it encompasses all three articles of the Creed.

The proposal of three kinds of righteousness is ultimately for the purpose of arguing that virtue ethics is a consistent manner in which to speak of ethical questions in a Lutheran framework. Biermann argues, in contrast to popular conceptions, that an Aristotelian model of ethics is not negated by the Lutheran emphasis on God's justifying word. Melanchthon and Luther's critique of Aristotle was not an attack on virtue ethics *per se*; rather, the problem with the medieval church was that virtue was seen as a path to justification. Biermann argues, "The two distinct righteousnesses had been collapsed into one. Aristotle and his practical truth had been adopted as the single structuring frame for all of life."[82] Because of this confusion, love, which is intended as the foundation for horizontal righteousness, was viewed with the saving efficacy that only faith has.[83] Aristotle's genuine insights into the moral life, therefore, need not be completely discarded in order for one to remain genuinely Lutheran in practice and ideology. Neither, however, must Aristotle have precedence over the biblical text itself, nor must his idea of virtue replace the chief article of the Christian faith, that the human creature is justified passively by faith alone. Virtue ethics is a proper framework with which to speak about active righteousness. Within its proper sphere, virtue constitutes the life of the Christian *coram mundo*. Biermann explains that Christians do not cultivate virtue in order to merit righteousness before God, but because this is the reason for which God put people within the realm of creation. To live a virtuous life is to do God's will.[84] Aristotle's insights can be applied both in the realm of civic and formative righteousness, insofar as they grant helpful categories to explicate God's commandments in Scripture.

The explication of ethics, within a theological and philosophical framework, would be useless were it not utilized in the parish life of the church. Biermann finishes his book by explaining how his proposal of three kinds of righteousness can be a helpful framework within which the average Christian can and should function. He first discusses the role of the pastor. For decades, many Lutheran pastors have feared utilizing the pulpit

81. Ibid.
82. Ibid., 153.
83. Ibid.
84. Ibid., 156.

to discuss moral issues due to their reticence to speak of anything other than the chief article of justification and the *coram Deo* relationship. In contradistinction to this, Biermann argues that "Christian people need to be trained in virtue."[85] This is part of the role of the pastor, and it should happen alongside of catechesis. The training of the people (and not simply in confirmation classes) should include both doctrinal and ethical instruction. These are both essential aspects of Christian education.

The community also plays an essential role in the formation of character. The believer does not develop virtue spontaneously, or on his own, but within the church. Biermann notes that a congregation serves as a community in which virtue can be cultivated by individual members.[86] As members of a congregation develop and cultivate their own virtuous character, they make their gospel witness more credible. The ethical character of the church is not, then, a distraction from gospel-proclamation, but defends and propels it.[87] The community of the church cultivates virtue by modeling it to other members of the congregation, as well as spending a significant amount of time teaching about specific ethical issues. In doing this, the church models what is means to be fully human as "it is Christ who perfectly exemplifies what it means to be fully human."[88] These virtues do not simply include actions which are directly pertinent to the neighbor, but also include "spiritual habits such as daily prayer (yes, even the use of rote, memorized prayers), regular use of the liturgy, making the sign of the cross, and a prominently emphasized church year."[89] When all of this occurs, the church is strengthened, and the witness of the gospel is extended.

Biermann's proposal is attractive for several reasons. First, he rightly emphasizes the inadequacy of the law-and-gospel framework as an overarching theological paradigm which explains everything there is to know about Christian doctrine and life. He demonstrates the flaws in the approach of theologians such as Gerhard Forde who decry any extended discussion of the incipient righteousness of the Christian. Second, Biermann gives preachers a helpful way to preach about the text, regardless of whether or not the text speaks explicitly in a law-gospel manner. Because of the three kinds of righteousness, the preacher is not constricted to a

---

85. Ibid., 191.
86. Ibid., 192.
87. Ibid., 193.
88. Ibid., 195.
89. Ibid., 196.

simplistic law-gospel structure for each sermon, but is free to use other frameworks in accord with the particular text in question. Third, Biermann corrects the flaw inherent in a two-kinds-of-righteousness approach. If the righteousness of the Christian and that of the unbeliever are not distinguished, then it would be easy for one to simply ignore active righteousness in preaching (why not if someone can hear it anywhere else?). Also, this omission neglects to take into account the biblical teaching of regeneration. Through regeneration, the believer gains spiritual impulses to do good. The believer lives in a special relationship to the law which the unbeliever does not. The difference is not simply in the fact that the believer is forgiven for his mistakes, but also in that the Christian begins to fulfill the law by grace.

Though Biermann's proposal is a positive one, and he solves many problems inherent in the law-gospel-reductionist paradigm of twentieth-century Lutheranism, there is one important missing factor from his work: the indwelling of the Holy Trinity. Biermann rightly emphasizes the external law given to both believers and unbelievers, and the central reality of faith, but he neglects any extensive discussion of the indwelling of God within the Christian. This is especially significant because this is the manner in which the Formula of Concord speaks of the two kinds of righteousness: one being the imputed righteousness of Christ, and the other being the indwelling of the divine nature, through which one's nature and will is renovated.

Of all three books examined in this chapter, Biermann's proposal is the most compelling. He presents a comprehensive case for the cultivation of virtue within a faithfully Lutheran framework. His distinction between three kinds of righteousness as opposed to the two kinds of righteousness solves several of the problems inherent in a two-kinds-of-righteousness framework. By distinguishing between governing and conforming righteousness, Biermann makes the case for a specifically Christian ethical system, avoiding the possible implication that active righteousness is exclusively confined to the civil sphere, and thus should not be central in Christian proclamation and catechesis. He also helpfully expounds upon the role of Aristotelianism in early Lutheranism and gives a helpful historical treatment, by way of the Lutheran Confessions, of the development of the two-kinds-of-righteousness idea in Luther and Melanchthon. Most importantly, Biermman gives a framework in which pastors can function to both cultivate Christian virtue and continue to emphasize justification by grace alone as the central reality of the Christian faith.

Though there are no significant theological problems in what is stated in Biermann's work, there are a few areas which could be helpfully expounded upon. This leads us to some of the primary concerns of this present book. While Biermann does distinguish between the civil righteousness of the unbeliever and the actual righteousness of the Christian, he does not sufficiently explain the nature of the relationship between these kinds of righteousness. What is missing in his treatment is the mystical union and the renewal of the *imago Dei*. Both of these concepts are consistently taught, both in Luther and the later Lutheran tradition, within the context of the active righteousness of the Christian. Secondly, though Biermann does acknowledge the importance of Christian piety (i.e., the first table of the law), he does not explain how this relates to the common horizontal/vertical explication of the two kinds of righteousness.

## Conclusion

Each of these three works has contributed some important explanations and clarifications regarding Luther's theme of the two kinds of righteousness. Wingren rightly emphasizes the distinction between the earthly and heavenly realms, and the nature of Luther's doctrine of vocation within the Christian's horizontal existence. Kolb and Arand demonstrate that the distinction between these two kinds of righteousness has implications in terms of the Christian's worldview and relationships. Biermann demonstrates how the three-kinds-of-righteousness paradigm helps to guard against antinomianism and gives pastors a Lutheran framework in which they can proclaim the necessity of good works and ethical formation.

There are two important aspect of Luther's teaching of the three kinds of righteousness which are absent in all of these writings. The first is one's union with Christ, which I have labeled "Christification" elsewhere; Christ is not only *extra nos* (as in justification) but is *intra nos* in our sanctification. Christ lives his own life in and through believers, as they are conformed to his image, which ultimately results in eschatological glorification and union with God. Second, none of the three sources explain the nature of the first table of the law and the place that love toward God has in this system. When Wingren's doctrine of vocation, Kolb and Arand's proposal of active righteousness before the world, and Biermann's argument for ethical formation are combined with the doctrine of union with Christ and an explanation of Eucharistic sacrifice toward God, a more complete picture of Luther's perspective on the Christian life can be seen. What follows is not an attempt to reject these previous proposals, but to build upon their foundation by demonstrating the importance of these themes in this ongoing discussion.

# Two Kinds of Righteousness in Luther's Theology

The distinction between the two kinds of righteousness, like most Lutheran distinctives, has its origin in Martin Luther's thought. In contrast to popular misconceptions, the sixteenth-century reformer was concerned with the proper role of both faith *and* works in the Christian life. Luther is a theologian of both law and gospel, justification and sanctification, active righteousness and passive righteousness. One of the ways in which Luther explores the connection between these vital aspects of the Christian life is in terms of the two kinds of righteousness. Luther's thought does, in many ways, correspond to contemporary proposals of the twofold righteousness, though there are important differences, as will be demonstrated. In this chapter, I have chosen to employ five specific sources. First are the sermons given by Luther entitled "Two Kinds of Righteousness" and "On Threefold Righteousness." These are the texts in which the language of the two kinds of righteousness is first utilized. The third text is Luther's treatise *Against Latomus*, in which he distinguishes between Christ as the favor of God and the gift of God. Fourth, I will examine Luther's famous Reformation treatise *On Christian Liberty*, which shows the place of the two kinds of righteousness within his central Reformation writings. Finally, Luther's 1535 Galatians commentary will be expounded upon, demonstrating that the theme of the twofold righteousness extends throughout his career.

Throughout this examination, four particular realities about Luther's thought are apparent. First, the two kinds of righteousness is not simply an occasional theme in Luther's thought, but it is a consistent emphasis throughout his career. Second, Luther is not simply a theologian of faith, but also of love. As Wingren contends, a one-sided emphasis on justification in Luther research has resulted in the loss of Luther's concept of love and good deeds. Third, union with Christ is an essential element of Luther's conception of both passive and active righteousness. This is a neglected theme in other explications of his thought on this subject. Finally, there are certain manners in which Luther's thought on this topic differ from contemporary proposals. Though he emphasizes the horizontal reality of Christian obedience, Luther does not limit it to such. He also, at times, speaks about divine indwelling and renovation as an aspect of passive righteousness, whereas the later Lutheran tradition explicitly distinguishes these two. One further difference is that Luther does not explain this distinction in the context of anthropology and human identity.

## *"The Two Kinds of Righteousness" (1518)*

The theme of the two kinds of righteousness first appears in Luther's sermon with that title. In this message, Luther expounds upon two separate kinds of righteousness: first is the alien righteousness of Christ, and second is the righteousness of the Christian, demonstrated in concrete action. This sermon, first preached in 1518, lays the groundwork for the development of this idea in Luther's thought and in the tradition which bears his name. When examined, it becomes apparent that what Luther means by "two kinds of righteousness" is not exactly what contemporary interpreters have contended, though there are several conceptual similarities.

Luther sets up the two kinds of righteousness within the context of two kinds of sin: original and actual. Original sin is the sin of Adam, which occurs apart from and outside of us. However, God still counts this sin to us, and this sin has grave consequences in the lives of all human creatures. Actual sin, on the other hand, refers to the specific sins of individuals as they live out their daily lives. This is a result of original sin, but the two are distinct. Luther asserts that corresponding to original sin, the first kind of righteousness is "alien righteousness, that is the righteousness of another, instilled from without. This is the righteousness of Christ by which he justifies through faith."[1] This passive righteousness is given through repentance and Holy Baptism.[2] Luther connects passive righteousness to the marriage union of faith, wherein the relationship between Christ and his church mirrors the relationship between a bride and her groom.[3] This theme of union with Christ in faith is a consistent theme in Luther's

---

1. *AE* 31:297.
2. Ibid.
3. Ibid.

theology of passive righteousness, as will be apparent when examining his later works on the subject.

For Luther, alien righteousness is not an attribute of Christ, but is, in a sense, Christ himself: "Through faith in Christ, therefore, Christ's righteousness becomes our righteousness and all that he has becomes ours; rather, he himself becomes ours."[4] He expresses the same sentiment again, writing, "he is entirely ours with all his benefits if we believe in him."[5] Luther does not distinguish between Christ's person and work, as do some contemporary theologies, but he instead argues that faith grasps Christ himself, and in doing so receives his benefits, including (but not limited to) his perfect righteousness. The content of this righteousness is not, as Osiander contended, simply Christ's divinity, but the historical acts of redemption which he accomplished. Luther specifically mentions Christ's "living, doing, and speaking, his suffering and dying."[6] Passive righteousness is thus received solely by faith, and this passive righteousness consists in both Christ's person *and* work.

Passive righteousness is described by Luther as "an infinite righteousness" which "swallows up all sins in a moment."[7] One is said to have this infinite righteousness because he "exists in Christ," and he is "one with Christ," again demonstrating the importance of union-with-Christ language in Luther.[8] The passive righteousness which one receives in union with Christ is the basis for active righteousness. It is primary in Christian proclamation, and is also foundation and cause of the Christian's active righteousness in the world.[9] Just as original sin serves as the basis for all actual sin, so does passive righteousness function as the basis for actual righteousness. Yet, this alien righteousness is not, for Luther, purely synonymous with forensic justification. For example, Luther argues that alien righteousness is not simply received once for all time. Instead, it progresses within the Christian, only to find its fulfillment in death.[10] This statement demonstrates two important points: First, at this stage in his career, Luther does not differentiate between imputed righteousness and the righteousness

4. Ibid., 298.
5. Ibid.
6. Ibid., 297.
7. Ibid., 298.
8. Ibid.
9. Ibid.
10. Ibid., 299.

of Christ within the believer, whereby one's union with Christ grows. In contradistinction to this, the Formula of Concord would later distinguish between imputed righteousness of Christ in justification, and the growing presence and work of Christ in sanctification, by placing the latter in the "active righteousness" category. Second, when Luther refers to "alien righteousness," he is not speaking in a locative manner, as if Christ's righteousness is spatially apart from us. Instead, he is speaking of its origin in Christ, rather than in the believer.

The second kind of righteousness, as explained by Luther, is the "manner of life spent profitably in good works."[11] This righteousness is not alien or passive, as is the first, but involves the actual obedient actions of the Christian. The central reality of this second kind of righteousness is love toward the neighbor. Through incipient righteousness, one is conformed to the image of Christ, while also attempting to be obedient to his example.[12] For Luther then, Christ is not only the favor of God, but is also both *donum* and *exemplar*. This second kind of righteousness is primarily a horizontal righteousness, referring to one's relationship to fellow human persons. In "each sphere" (a synonym for vocation), the believer is to seek the welfare of others as Christ acted for the welfare of the human race.[13] However, this second kind of righteousness is not limited to its horizontal dimensions. It is involves living "devoutly toward God."[14] This kind of righteousness is also not concerned purely with external good works which serve the neighbor, but also "slaying the flesh,"[15] and striving to "do away with the body of Adam and to destroy the body of sin."[16] Thus the whole life of sanctified living, including love toward neighbor, devotion to God, and the killing of sin, are aspects of active righteousness.[17]

11. Ibid.

12. "This righteousness follows the example of Christ in this respect and is transformed into his likeness" (ibid., 300).

13. Ibid.

14. Ibid., 299.

15. Ibid.

16. Ibid., 300.

17. Kolb contends, regarding the development of the two-kinds-of-righteousness theme in Luther's thought, that "Luther realized, however, that what made him genuinely right in God's sight had to be distinguished from what made him truly human—genuinely right—in relationship to other creatures of God" ("Luther on Two Kinds," 451). There is no language of active righteousness making one "truly human" in this sermon, or any other treatment of the two kinds of righteousness. The contention is unfounded

Luther uses extensive union language in reference to the second kind of righteousness in the same manner that he does with the first. The first kind of righteousness refers to the bond which the husband (Christ) establishes with the bride (the soul). The second kind of righteousness is then the bride's response to the bridegroom: "I am yours."[18] In response to the love of Christ, the believer then, secure in his righteousness before God, looks only to the well-being of the neighbor.[19] The welfare which one seeks for others is based upon the grace that Christ showed to sinners. Thus the first kind of righteousness serves as the motive, power, and model of the second. Active righteousness is always rooted in the work of Christ *pro nobis*.

The two kinds of righteousness, as expounded upon by Luther in this sermon, are passive righteousness and active righteousness. There are several differences, however, between how Luther explains both of these concepts and how they are defined by Kolb, Arand, and Biermann. Passive righteousness refers primarily to justification: the forgiveness of sins and the imputation of righteousness. However, Luther also includes transitive renovation as an aspect of passive righteousness. This includes all that God does for and in the believer which is passively received, including the forgiveness of sins as well as the growth of alien righteousness *within* the believer. Active righteousness then refers to the moral actions of the believer in accord with God's law. Though Luther focuses *primarily* on the works which serve the neighbor, he also includes one's vertical relationship with God.[20] The vertical/horizontal axis utilized by contemporary proponents of the two kinds of righteousness, as helpful as it may be, is not exhaustive of Luther's teaching here.[21] One final point to be made regarding this

---

within Luther's early writings. Were this part of Luther's Reformation breakthrough, he would have been explicit about it at some point in his writings.

18. *AE* 31:300.

19. Ibid.

20. Arand and Biermann, for example, give the following definition of the two kinds of righteousness: "God created us as relational beings; and human relationships take place within two fundamental realms or arenas: we live before God (*coram Deo*), and before the world (*coram mundo*). These realms are inhabited simultaneously; we live in God's presence and at the same time in community with one another where we have responsibility for fellow creatures" ("Why the Two Kinds of Righteousness," 118). While Luther does speak in this way, especially when dealing with the two kingdoms, it is apparent that this is not quite what Luther means in this sermon by the distinction between the two kinds of righteousness.

21. Another problem with contemporary treatments of this sermon is that some writers have sought to extrapolate an entire ontological system from Luther's distinction.

sermon is that Luther speaks, not of civil righteousness, but of the renovation of the Christian in particular as active righteousness. This shows the importance of the distinction Biermann makes between civil and inchoate Christian righteousness when explaining Luther's thought. Though civil righteousness is a reality in Luther's theology, it differs from the proper acts of righteousness performed in faith.

## "On Threefold Righteousness" (1518)

Luther's sermon on threefold righteousness deals with the same topic as the previously discussed sermon, and is also based on Philippians 2. The textual similarities as well as the thematic parallels demonstrate that these sermons are somehow connected. There has been some debate regarding which sermon was preached first, and which document then serves as a revision of the other.[22] While these questions remain largely unanswered, what is apparent is that both of these sermons were preached by Luther and express his thoughts on the subject at hand. For the present purposes, it is enough to note that both of these sermons express Luther's early thought on the two kinds of righteousness.

The primary difference between this sermon and his earlier message, other than its brevity, is the additional discussion of civil righteousness. In this sermon, Luther again contrasts aspects of sin with aspects of righteousness. He asserts that some sin is considered "manifest evil," because this sin is recognized by Christian and non-Christian alike.[23] This type of sin is punished by the state. Luther cites the examples of theft, homicide, arson,

---

Kolb, for example, writes, "Luther's ontology recognized that reality springs from and rests upon what God says. This ontology of the Word convinced him that when God declares, 'forgiven,' he restores the original humanity of his chosen children" ("Luther on Two Kinds of Righteousness," 459). This type of language is simply absent from the sermon, which is not about theological anthropology, but the relationship between justification and good works. The general metaphysic that Luther is working with at this point is no different than that of his mystical forebears such as Tauler and the *Theologia Germanica*. Luther's language of alien righteousness growing within the Christian is consistent with earlier mystical writers who emphasize the life that Christ lives within the human subject.

22. Kolb places "Threefold Righteousness" first in early 1518, and argues that "Two Kinds of Righteousness" was preached in late 1518 or early 1519 based on the text of "Threefold Righteousness." Arand and Biermann follow this assessment in "Why the Two Kinds of Righteousness," 217.

23. Luther, "Threefold Righteousness."

and sacrilege.[24] In contrast to manifest evil, citizens of a commonwealth can have a type of civic righteousness. This righteousness is not necessarily Christian righteousness, because it belongs to the regenerate and unregenerate alike. This righteousness is rewarded with temporal blessings, such as in the instances of Namaan and the blessings given to the Roman Empire.[25] Luther argues that Christians should not seek to have this particular type of righteousness. The differentiating factor between civil righteousness and the righteous deeds of the Christian is that of motivation. Civil righteousness, unlike the Christian's active righteousness, is performed for self-glorification and fear of negative repercussions.[26] The righteous deeds of unbelievers are performed because of fear of punishment or for the hope of reward. Because of this, Christians are discouraged from this kind of righteousness "in favor of a better one."[27]

Secondly, Luther discusses passive righteousness. He again compares passive righteousness to the sin of Adam, calling original sin "essential sin, original, alien."[28] In the same way, the righteousness received by Christians is also alien, being the righteousness of Christ, in which one partakes through baptism.[29] This is the righteousness by which many are counted as righteous due to the obedience of Christ. This righteousness is received solely by faith and is opposed to the righteousness of the law. Luther explains this more fully by contrasting Adam and Christ:

> Fifthly, the Apostle says [Rom 5:14]: that Adam is the pattern of the future one, obviously in the same way that Adam by one sin, certainly alien to them, by that same sin, as properly their own sin, makes all born out of him answerable and gives them what he has, so Christ by means of His own righteousness, that same righteousness of his own, alien to them and unmerited, makes all those born out of him righteous and saved ones, so that, as we were damned by means of an alien sin, thus we might be freed by an alien righteousness.[30]

24. Ibid.
25. Ibid.
26. Ibid.
27. Ibid.
28. Ibid.
29. Ibid.
30. Ibid.

As Adam's sin is counted to all of his descendants, so is Christ's righteousness counted to all who are born in him. This righteousness is an eternal righteousness, which secures the salvation of all who believe.

The final kind of righteousness spoken of by Luther in this text is active righteousness. Just as there are personal sins, so are there also personal righteous actions. This active righteousness arises from the reality of faith, and the passive righteousness received.[31] This active righteousness involves one's renewal in the *imago Dei*. This third kind of righteousness is in no way meritorious, because Christ's merit is received solely by faith apart from works. Luther does not, as in the previous sermon, give extensive explanations as to what this third kind of righteousness looks like in the life of the Christian. He briefly mentions "prayers, alms, fasting, finally [Rom 12] most beautifully of all things, and elsewhere: Mortify your members [Col 3:5]. Because from that third righteousness nothing else is sought, than that original sin be overcome, and the body of sin destroyed, and thus the reigning righteousness itself be a merit, not however because the act have a reward, but only advances the merit."[32] These good deeds are set in contrast to self-made works which were prominent in the medieval church.

This sermon roughly corresponds to Biermann's proposal of the three kinds of righteousness, including civil, passive, and active righteousness. Luther makes the necessary important distinction between the first and third kinds of righteousness. Good works are different between the believer and unbeliever concerning the reality of faith and the motive behind the works performed. Luther does not mention growth in alien righteousness as he does in "Two Kinds of Righteousness," but focuses instead narrowly on imputation. The horizontal aspect of good works is missing here, unlike in his previous sermon, as he instead focuses on prayer, fasting, and the mortification of sin. This is likely due to the brevity of this particular writing. It, does, however, demonstrate the importance of the first table of the law within Christian living.

## Christ as Favor and Donum

Another manner in which Luther speaks about the distinction between two kinds of righteousness is the distinction made between Christ as God's favor toward the sinner, as well as God's gift to the sinner. God's favor refers

31. Ibid.
32. Ibid.

to his forgiving of sins, and the language of gift corresponds to the healing of human nature through the indwelling Christ. This distinction, explained in his treatise *Against Latomus*, is a further explication of the two kinds of righteousness given to the Christian.

Luther posits that there are two aspects of the gospel: the righteousness of God and the grace of God.[33] Righteousness roughly corresponds to regeneration and sanctification. Luther notes, "Almost always in Scripture, this righteousness which is contrary to sin refers to an innermost root whose fruits are good works."[34] Righteousness is that which truly changes the Christian inwardly, and thus bears the fruit of good deeds. The second gift of the gospel is God's grace, which Luther defines as "the good will [*favor*] of God, against wrath which is the partner of sin, so that he who believes in Christ has a merciful God."[35] Luther explains that this distinction can also be described in terms of the difference between faith and grace. He argues that the forgiveness of sins and peace with God are results of the grace of God, wherein healing from the corruption of sin is the result of faith.[36] Salvation has a twofold benefit: the remission of sins and the healing from sin. For Luther, both aspects comprise the gospel. The mortification of sin and Christian obedience are not neglected by Luther, but must be differentiated from justifying righteousness.

The gifts of the gospel correspond to the "evils of the law."[37] The gift is given because of sin, and grace is given because of wrath. Wrath and grace are both external realities. They refer to God's disposition toward an individual rather than something within the person. Because the person is holistic, wrath and grace are complete realities. One cannot be partially under wrath and partially under grace. Luther contends, "He whom God receives in grace, He completely receives, and he whom He favors, He completely favors. On the other hand, He is angry at the whole of him with whom He is angry."[38] It is in this sense that Luther can speak of the Christian being *simul iustus et peccator* in a *totus/totus* manner, as do Kolb and Arand. Under the law, which in its strict judgment does not differentiate between breaking one or all of its commandments, the human creature

33. *AE* 32:227.
34. Ibid.
35. Ibid.
36. Ibid.
37. Ibid., 228.
38. Ibid.

is totally under the wrath of God, and is thus totally sinner. Under grace, which forgives and covers every sin, one is then completely righteous. But when speaking about the gift, Luther argues differently. In contemporary terminology one could say that *coram deo*, one is total saint–total sinner, and *coram mundo*, one is part saint–part sinner. Kolb and Arand are thus consistent with Luther in emphasizing the total character of the Christian's nature as sinner and saint, but they are misreading Luther in disallowing a *partim/partim* manner of speaking, which is also in accord with Luther's theology. Each simply needs to be placed within its proper sphere.

The Christian has both the grace of God and the gift of God; the believer is set free from the twofold effect of sin: guilt and corruption.[39] While God's grace covers over man's sin, so that he is completely and entirely righteous in his sight, the gift "heals from sin and from his corruption of body and soul."[40] Luther expounds upon the nature of the gift: "The gift has been infused, the leaven has been added to the mixture."[41] It is particularly noteworthy, at this point in Luther's career, that he remains comfortable with the language of infusion, so long as that language is distanced from *coram Deo* salvation. Even though one is perfectly righteous under grace, the power of sin is not taken away all at once. It is in this sense that the Christian can be said to be partly saint and partly sinner. Through the gift, sin is gradually "purged away."[42] Luther likens this process to the vinedresser who gradually prunes the vine, thus causing the vine to bear more fruit. Through the gift of faith, the old Adam is destroyed. This happens, not simply by the ceasing of particular sins (though that is certainly a result), but by killing the root of sin. In doing this, God does not only cause the regenerate person to cease committing particular sins, but the person himself is changed through renewal.[43] These faults cease in the slow process of pruning, by which the Christian can rightly be said to be in a process of spiritual growth. It might be said that sanctification and good works are not identical for Luther, but good works are the external fruit of the inward reality of renewal.

There are some slight differences between this treatment of the double benefit of the gospel and Luther's earlier discussions about the two kinds of

39. Ibid., 229.
40. Ibid.
41. Ibid.
42. Ibid., 230.
43. Ibid., 233.

righteousness. In "Two Kinds of Righteousness," Luther includes both the imputation of righteousness and growth in alien righteousness under the category of "passive righteousness." Active righteousness is, then, the fruit of good works which flows from this passive righteousness. In this treatise, Luther distinguishes more sharply between the forensic aspect of salvation (grace) and the renovative aspects (*donum*). This sharp distinction between forensic passive righteousness and transformative active righteousness, expounded here in 1521, would characterize later Lutheran treatments of the subject. It is a much more clear and comprehensive division than his previous differentiation between active and passive righteousness, which at times, conflates the forensic and renovative acts of God.

## The Freedom of a Christian

In one of his three great Reformation treatises of 1520, *The Freedom of a Christian*, Luther continues to expound upon the relationship between justification and good works in the Christian life. Though he does not explicitly use the terminology of the "two kinds of righteousness," nor of the "favor and gift," his argument is essentially the same: God gives salvation as a free gift of grace, to be received by faith alone. This faith is then operative in the world as one kills sin and serves the neighbor in love.

Luther expounds upon Christian liberty with the two following statements, which roughly correspond to the distinction between passive and active righteousness: A Christian is a perfectly free lord of all, subject to none (passive righteousness). A Christian is a perfectly dutiful servant of all, subject to all (active righteousness).[44] Though these two statements appear to be contradictory, they both refer to separate aspects of man's being in the world.[45] Luther notes that the human creature has a dual nature. One is comprised of both body and soul.[46] Luther contends that there are several statements in Scripture which seem contradictory to one another because they address one or another part of the human person. Righteousness, or justification, is concerned with the spiritual nature of man, because external realities do not produce, or effect in any way, true Christian righteousness.[47] Rather, the gospel is a spiritual matter which must be received

44. *AE* 31:344.
45. Ibid.
46. Ibid.
47. Ibid., 345.

by the soul. Mere external acceptance of the gospel with one's mouth, if one's heart does not trust, is irrelevant to personal salvation. The soul simply needs the gospel as granted through the word as an efficacious means of salvation.[48]

The soul does not need any works. Rather, it simply needs the divine word, through which righteousness is granted and faith is created.[49] Works do no benefit to the soul. It is in this matter that the law and the gospel must be strictly distinguished. Though the divine commandments are holy, righteous, and good, they are given primarily for the purpose that one might realize the reality of one's sin and inability to perform righteousness.[50] In one's *coram Deo* relationship, within the soul, the law serves purely to drive one to a knowledge of one's inability to fulfill it, and thus to Christ's own righteousness. This second use, as it would later be labeled, is the central use of the divine law for Luther, especially in reference to the divine-human relationship. The gospel, in contrast to the law, says, "If you believe, you shall have all things."[51] It belongs to God both to give commandments and also to fulfill these same commandments. This is how the law and the gospel are commensurate with one another. When hearing God's promises, the soul is "so closely united with them and altogether absorbed by them that it not only will share in all their power but will be saturated and intoxicated by them."[52] As in "Two Kinds of Righteousness," Luther speaks of passive righteousness in the context of the union of faith, whereby the believing subject and Christ are brought together in a marriage bond. This union is based solely on faith, and not in any way upon works, which do not have their abode in the soul, but rather live in the body.[53]

Luther gives an extensive explanation of the nature of this marriage union. He notes that faith connects the soul to Christ as a bride and groom are united through the bond of marriage.[54] In this union, Christ and the soul become one flesh, and in this bond a great exchange occurs. Luther explains:

48. Ibid.
49. Ibid., 346.
50. Ibid., 348.
51. Ibid., 348–49.
52. Ibid., 349.
53. Ibid.
54. Ibid., 351.

> Christ is full of grace, life, and salvation. The soul is full of sins, death, and damnation. Now let faith come between them and sins, death, and damnation will be Christ's, while grace, life, and salvation will be the soul's; for if Christ is a bridegroom, he must take upon himself the things which are his bride's and bestow upon her the things that are his. If he gives her his body and his very self, how shall he not give her all that is his? And if he takes the body of the bride, how shall he not take all that is hers?[55]

This union is not a renovative one (what Lutheran orthodoxy called the *unio mystica*), but an imputational one.[56] In the relationship established between Christ and the soul, which arises solely by faith, Christ takes the believer's sins upon himself, and grants his righteousness to the Christian. This is how the Christian is justified *coram Deo*.

Because of this marriage bond of faith, the believer "rules over all things, death, life, and sin," and he consequently performs good works.[57] Luther's thesis statement, that the Christian is "Lord of all things, subject to none," is explained in light of the doctrine of justification. The believer has no need of works to avail for righteousness and salvation, because that is the distinctive characteristic of faith.[58] In the realm of justification, good works play absolutely no role whatsoever. In fact, good works can even be harmful to the soul if one trusts in them for salvation. Thus, in the realm in which man stands before God, as a soul, works play no role whatever. Instead, it is only faith that has any relevance, because faith unites one with Christ and receives his benefits.

After expounding upon his first thesis, Luther proceeds to discuss his second, that the Christian is a "dutiful servant to all, subject to all." Here, Luther speaks about "the outer man." According to his relationship before God, the Christian "does no works," but as a servant he "does all kinds of works."[59] These works are necessary because of the bodily nature of human existence. On earth is where good works are essential. Luther explains that the Christian's earthly life cannot be leisurely, but must be strictly devoted to Christian discipline, that he might slay the sin which dwells within

---

55. Ibid.

56. This is what David Hollaz refers to as the *unio fidei formalis*, the formal union of faith.

57. *AE* 31:355.

58. Ibid., 356.

59. Ibid., 358.

him.[60] As one lives in a body, and since the body is enticed by various lusts, the Christian must keep watch over his body so that it is used for God's purposes. Here, spiritual disciplines are an absolute necessity, as one seeks to suppress the lusts of the flesh. The good works done in the body are performed out of love for God, and in response to God's grace; they are never performed in order to gain justification.[61]

The faith and intention behind a good work are essential to determining the goodness of any particular work. The unbeliever performs works in order to save himself before God, but the Christian has achieved salvation already, in Christ, and thus performs good deeds in order to please his Heavenly Father, through whom one has already been reconciled.[62] If one does works, in contrast to this, for personal salvation, the work is no longer a good deed, but is instead damnable. The passive righteousness of faith stands behind every good work that the Christian performs, and those works are only good and acceptable to God because of faith in Christ.

Luther argues that good works are largely a horizontal enterprise. They are done for the sake of others. He argues that "A man does not live for himself alone in this mortal body to work for it alone, but he lives also for all men on earth; rather, he lives only for others and not for himself."[63] This is the first instance wherein Luther explicitly refers to active righteousness as a horizontal reality, as do contemporary proponents of the two kinds of righteousness. He even views the subjection of the body, as he speaks of earlier in discussing fasting and other spiritual disciplines, as something done for the sake of the neighbor.[64] He later says that concern for the neighbor is the "one thing alone" that should guide the Christian's good works.[65] According to Luther, this is precisely what Paul means when speaking about the faith which works through love (Gal 5:6).

The Christian's good works for his neighbor are a reflection of the works which Christ has done for him. As Christ has done, the believer is called to take the form of a servant and treat the neighbor in the same

60. Ibid.

61. Ibid., 359.

62. Ibid., 362.

63. Ibid., 364.

64. "To this end he brings his body into subjection that he may the more sincerely and freely serve others" (ibid.).

65. Ibid., 365.

manner that Christ has dealt with sinners.[66] In doing this, we become Christ to our neighbor, and Christ works through us for the good of others. Luther argues that divine indwelling is an essential aspect of this active righteousness that Christians have before the world. He writes, "Surely we are named after Christ, not because he is absent from us, but because he dwells in us, that is, because we believe in him and are Christs one to another and do to our neighbor as Christ does to us."[67] Christ lives in and through the believer, and because of this the Christian is conformed to his image. This also demonstrates the importance of one's union with Christ, not only in passive righteousness, but also in active righteousness. One must distinguish here between the marriage union of faith, through which the benefits of Christ are imputed to the Christian, and the indwelling of Christ, wherein the believer is changed and renewed in God's image. As there are two kinds of righteousness, so also there are two kinds of union corresponding to each.[68]

The essence of the Christian's relationship to the world is love. All good works are done, not for the sake of self-justification, but instead "joyfully for the sake of others."[69] The freedom one has from the condemnation of the law in free justification does not give one license to sin; rather, it frees one to be able to perform good works for the sake of the neighbor, rather than obsessing over one's own salvation. Luther expresses the relationship between the faith which receives Christ and the love which serves the neighbor in the following manner: "We conclude therefore, that a Christian lives not in himself, but in Christ and in his neighbor. Otherwise he is not a Christian. He lives in Christ through faith, in his neighbor through love. By faith he is caught up beyond himself into God. By love he descends beneath himself into his neighbor."[70] Wingren is correct in interpreting Luther here; both faith and love are essential and they operate in different spheres. Faith receives the righteousness of Christ *coram Deo*, and love serves the neighbor *coram mundo*.

Though the exact phrase is not utilized in this work, it is apparent that Luther's theme of the two kinds of righteousness underlies the theology

66. Ibid., 366.

67. Ibid., 368.

68. This is what David Hollaz calls the *unio fidei formalis* and the *unio mystica*, as will be explained below.

69. *AE* 31:368.

70. Ibid., 371.

of *The Freedom of a Christian*. Regarding one's relationship before God, according to the soul, the believer is perfectly free from all works, being justified solely by faith. Before the world, one is subject to serve all people in love, not to justify oneself, but in response to what Christ has done, and through Christ's indwelling. Active righteousness consists in the believer's good works in the world for the neighbor, which occurs through the indwelling of Christ.

## Active and Passive Righteousness in the Commentary on Galatians (1535)

In his monumental commentary on Paul's letter to the Galatians, Luther expounds heavily upon the theme of the two kinds of righteousness. Throughout the work, Luther carefully distinguishes between passive righteousness and the various forms of active righteousness, demonstrating both the centrality of passive righteousness and the importance of active righteousness in the world. It is clear in this work that the themes developed in his early writings on this topic are an essential part of Luther's thought throughout his life.

In the introduction, Luther explains the central thesis of Paul's letter and of his commentary. His thesis statement is as follows: "Paul wants to establish the doctrine of faith, grace, the forgiveness of sins or Christian righteousness, so that we may have a perfect knowledge and know the difference between Christian righteousness and all other kinds of righteousness."[71] By Christian righteousness, Luther means passive or alien righteousness, or that which makes one a Christian. He then expounds upon exactly what the "other kinds of righteousness" are: political (i.e., civic righteousness), ceremonial righteousness, and the righteousness of the Decalogue. This final kind of righteousness is not rejected by Luther, but he states that this is only taught following justification by faith.[72] Thus Luther views the law as important, not simply in order to show people their sin prior to hearing the gospel, but also to guide people in life after hearing the gospel.

Luther is very careful to distinguish between passive and active righteousness without negating the importance of one's active righteousness in the world. Speaking of the different kinds of active righteousness, Luther

71. *AE* 26:4.
72. Ibid.

writes that the various forms of active righteousness are also divine gifts.[73] Though they are important, these various kinds of active righteousness are the opposite of passive righteousness. Regarding the passive righteousness which justifies, "We work nothing, render nothing to God; we only receive and permit someone else to work in us, namely, God."[74] It is this, and only this, passive righteousness which matters in justification. Luther can even say, "I do not seek active righteousness."[75] In perhaps an even more extreme statement, Luther writes, "It is a marvelous thing and unknown to the world to teach Christians to ignore the Law and to live before God as though there were no Law whatever."[76] These kinds of statements might lead one to believe that the law and active righteousness have no relevance in the Christian life. This however would contradict several other statements in his writings. In fact, just after he argues that he does not seek active righteousness, he notes, "I ought to have it [active righteousness] and perform it."[77] The solution to this dilemma is recognizing the important distinction between one's *coram Deo* and *coram mundo* relationships. In one's standing before God, law is irrelevant; in one's place in society, the law is essential.

Luther demonstrates that his primary concern is for people to properly distinguish between the two kinds of righteousness. He writes,

> For if I were to teach men the Law in such a way that they suppose themselves to be justified by it before God, I would be going beyond the limit of the Law, confusing these two righteousnesses, the active and the passive, and would be a bad dialectician who does not properly distinguish. But when I go beyond the old man, I also go beyond the Law. For the flesh or the old man, the Law and works, are all joined together. In the same way the spirit or the new man is joined to the promise and to grace.[78]

This is similar to the distinction Luther makes in *On Christian Liberty*, wherein according to the Spirit, through justification, one is the servant of none, and according to the body, in concrete living in the world, one is a servant of all.

73. Ibid.
74. Ibid., 5.
75. Ibid., 6.
76. Ibid.
77. Ibid.
78. Ibid., 7.

Luther refers to the distinction between passive and active righteousness as "our theology."[79] This distinction is not merely incidental in Luther, but is at the heart of the theology of the Lutheran Reformation. On the one hand, Luther lists active righteousness, which includes morality, works, and secular society. On the other, he defines passive righteousness as "faith, grace, and religion." Luther argues that both of these "righteousnesses" are necessary, but within their proper spheres; the law applies to the old man, and the gospel to the new.[80] Active righteousness applies to the earth, and to the good works which must be performed for the sake of others. Passive righteousness is about heaven, and here good works and the law are unnecessary. When these two kinds of righteousness are conflated, heaven and earth are confused, and one inevitably will "relapse into active righteousness [for justification]; that is, when he has lost Christ, he must fall into a trust in his own works."[81] It is necessary for the clear proclamation of the gospel for these kinds of righteousness to be distinguished.[82]

Luther does not view passive righteousness simply as an external declaration of justification which has no effect within the sinner. Instead, the passive righteousness of faith is the cause of good works within the Christian. He writes,

> When I have this righteousness within me, I descend from heaven like the rain that makes the earth fertile. That is, I come forth into another kingdom, and I perform good works whenever the opportunity arises. If I am a minister of the Word, I preach, I comfort the saddened, I administer the sacraments. If I am a father, I rule my household and family, I train my children in piety and honesty. If I am a magistrate, I perform the office which I have received by divine command. If I am a servant, I faithfully tend to my master's affairs. In short, whoever knows for sure that Christ is his

79. Ibid.

80. Ibid.

81. Ibid., 9.

82. Luther does not, however, utilize the distinction here to explain what it means to be "fully human." Kolb argues, "Also central to Luther's 'evangelical breakthrough' was his discovery of what makes the human creature 'righteous' or right, that is, truly human. This involves the distinction emphasized in the preface to the 1535 Galatians commentary cited above" ("Luther on the Two Kinds of Righteousness," 450). There is no mention in this entire context of the definition of what constitutes humanity, nor is there in any of Luther's treatment of the two kinds of righteousness. To argue that the distinction between the two kinds of righteousness constitutes a Lutheran anthropology goes beyond the intention of Luther.

righteousness not only cheerfully and gladly works in his calling but also submits himself for the sake of love to magistrates, also to their wicked laws, and to everything else in this present life—even, if need be, to burden and danger. For he knows that God wants this and that this obedience pleases him.[83]

Passive and active righteousness do intersect for Luther. The righteousness received by the Christian from heaven is brought down into the horizontal realm.[84] Here, the Christian performs the duties required of him according to his office.

Throughout his commentary, Luther is immensely critical of the *fides caritate formata* (faith formed by love) teaching of the medieval church.[85] To add love to faith in justification is to conflate these two kinds of righteousness. In contrast to this, "the Gospel is this, that our righteousness comes by faith alone, without the works of the Law."[86] To argue that such a faith must be supplemented by any virtue within the person, whether love or something else, is to place righteousness in the law rather than the gospel. The object of faith is not love, nor does faith justify because of the love it produces (though faith does produce love). Rather, faith justifies because it "takes hold of Christ, the Son of God, and is adorned by him."[87] Through faith, one takes hold of Christ himself and is thus imputed with his righteousness.

Wingren properly understands Luther's theology of civil righteousness—the "masks of God." Because humans cannot see God's face directly, one must see God according to his masks by which he works. Luther notes that a variety of positions in this world serve in this fashion, including "the magistrate, the emperor, the king, the prince, the consul, the teacher, the preacher, the pupil, the father, the mother, the children, the master, the servant."[88] In this way, God works through all people, whether regenerate or unregenerate, for the preservation of the world. In terms of

---

83. *AE* 26:12.

84. Arand and Biermann rightly contend that Christians are to be both: "totally passive—as a newborn child of God—and totally active—as a responsible neighbor to other people and to the whole of God's world" ("Why the Two Kinds," 120).

85. In this medieval teaching, faith is not viewed as saving unless it is formed by works of love by the Christian.

86. *AE* 26:88.

87. Ibid., 88–89.

88. Ibid., 95.

justification, God has "no regard" to one's earthly position.[89] However, in the broader world, our different stations in life are immensely important. Luther argues that "God wants us to honor and respect these 'positions' as His masks or instruments through which He preserves and governs the world."[90] Though civil righteousness does not necessarily constitute truly good works, because of the possible lack of faith within the person doing them, it is a genuinely important and necessary part of life *coram mundo*.

Luther frames the distinction between law and gospel within the framework of the two kinds of righteousness. He states that the two are to be distinguished in terms of the divergent realms in which they function: the law has its proper role on earth, and the gospel in heaven. The law is a human-human reality, and the gospel establishes the divine-human relationship.[91] Luther thus does not only differentiate between law and gospel in terms of condemnation and forgiveness, but also in view of the two kingdoms. Regarding faith and justification, Luther urges, "let us leave the Law out of consideration altogether and let it remain on the earth."[92] Luther's language regarding one's place in society is just as strong. Here, the law must be "strictly required."[93] In society, we should "let nothing be known about the Gospel, conscience, grace, the forgiveness of sins, heavenly righteousness, or Christ himself; but let there be knowledge only of Moses, of the Law and its works."[94] These two realms must always be distinguished. The law cannot rule in the conscience, nor can the gospel rule on the earth. This can even be stated in terms of two kinds of justification; Luther says that, "the Law justifies on earth and the Gospel in heaven."[95] When the conscience is troubled, one should look solely to the gospel. But when one is looking for guidance within one's vocation, he should look solely to the law.

89. Ibid., 96.
90. Ibid.
91. Ibid., 115.
92. Ibid.
93. Ibid., 116.
94. Ibid.
95. Ibid., 117.

## Union with Christ in the Galatians Commentary (1535)

The theme of union with Christ has been a prominent one in Luther scholarship since the publication of Tuomo Mannermaa's *Christ Present in Faith* in 1979, which argues for continuity between Luther's doctrine of union and the Eastern teaching of theosis. These studies have largely focused on the Galatians commentary. The theme of union will be discussed here only in relation to our present purposes of examining Luther's development of the theme of the two kinds of righteousness. Thus, readers should not expect an extensive discussion of the Eastern conception of theosis, as I have done elsewhere.[96] What will be demonstrated is that there is an extensive amount of "union with Christ" language in relation to both passive and active righteousness. Examining this theme in Luther's commentary will help to demonstrate the immense difference between the righteousness of the unbeliever (civic) and that of the Christian (intrinsic).

There are times in which Luther speaks about union within the context of justification, as Mannermaa has demonstrated. Luther writes,

> Here it is to be noted that these three things are joined together: faith, Christ, and acceptance or imputation. Faith takes hold of Christ and has Him present, enclosing Him as the ring encloses the gem. And whoever is found having this faith in the Christ who is grasped in the heart, him God accounts as righteous. This is the means and the merit by which we obtain the forgiveness of sins and righteousness. "Because you believe in Me," God says, "and your faith takes hold of Christ, whom I have freely given to you as your Justifier and Savior, therefore be righteous." Thus God accepts you or accounts you righteous only on account of Christ, in whom you believe.[97]

Luther argues that Christ is present in faith itself, and that through his presence in faith, as one is united with him, one is accounted as righteous. Luther thus does not place union solely in the active righteousness category; rather, he repeats his earlier contention that there is a marriage bond of faith with Christ which serves as the context for the great exchange, wherein Christ's righteousness is given to the sinner.

This union of faith is distinguished in Luther from the indwelling of Christ, wherein one is progressively sanctified and performs good works.

---

96. See Cooper, *Christification*.

97. *AE* 26, 132.

Luther urges that the Christian should love both God and neighbor due to one's union with Christ in faith.[98] Justifying faith is saving in and of itself, and because of the fact that it is accompanied by love and obedience; even though the preacher has a duty to teach on Christian obedience, it must not be discussed within the context of justification.[99] Instead, here the question is about what Christ has done, and the blessings which he bestows on the believer through faith.[100] It is here, in an explicit discussion of what distinguishes gospel from law, passive righteousness from active righteousness, that Luther says, "By faith we are in Him, and He is in us."[101] This intimate union which the believer has with Christ, wherein Christ gives his very self in marriage to the soul, is central to the gospel, not the law. Luther likens this union to the time a married couple spends alone immediately following the wedding. Following this is the reception, wherein others are served food and drink. This is where one begins to perform good deeds in love.[102] The marriage itself between Christ and the soul, which is through faith, is passive righteousness, or pure gospel, for Luther. The works of the believer then follow as a result, yet as a separate action of, this union.

Luther contends that after one "possesses Christ by faith, and knows that He is his righteousness and life, he will certainly not be idle but, like a sound tree, will bear good fruit."[103] The possession of Christ by faith (passive righteousness) leads to a life of good works, wherein Christ indwells and changes the believer (active righteousness). Luther agrees here with Rome that "faith without works is worthless and useless,"[104] but not because faith needs works to make it valid before God, but because true faith always necessarily produces works. If faith really unites one to Christ, then Christ is always going to change the one with whom he is in union. Luther contends that "faith without works—that is, a fantastic idea and mere vanity and a dream of the heart—is a false faith and does not justify."[105] Good works are done as a result of the passive righteousness which has been received. They are performed because the believer is made a new creation in Christ with

98. Ibid., 133.
99. Ibid., 137.
100. Ibid.
101. Ibid.
102. Ibid., 138.
103. Ibid., 155.
104. Ibid.
105. Ibid.

new desires, and out of the thankfulness of one's heart for the salvation gained. In this context, Luther reverses the "faith formed by love" terminology. Rather than love adorning and making faith saving, faith adorns and brings value to love.[106] Love is a necessary outcome of true saving faith, but it does not add salvific value to faith.

One might be tempted to argue here that the law need not be enforced upon the Christian, since love and good deeds are spontaneous. This is apparent when one focuses solely on the "motivation" question in ethical discourse, as Biermann has rightly demonstrated. Insofar as the believer is regenerated and renewed, he will perform good deeds joyfully and freely. The law will be fulfilled out of gratitude and without enticement. However, since believers are never freed from the flesh in this life, "the flesh must be disciplined by laws and vexed by the requirements and punishments of laws, as I have often admonished." In contradistinction to this, "the inner man, who owes nothing to the Law but is free of it, is a living, righteous, and holy person—not of himself or in his own substance but in Christ."[107] The Christian then must actually consciously try to live according to God's will by suppressing the old man. This happens even through threats and punishments.

Along with the union of faith which the believer has with Christ, there is also an extensive discussion of Christ's indwelling within the believer in Luther's writing. In one place, Luther defines Christian righteousness (which term he uses throughout to distinguish passive from active righteousness) as "that righteousness by which Christ lives in us, not the righteousness that is in our own person."[108] Here Luther defines justifying righteousness as Christ *in us*, not simply Christ *for us*. Luther is, again, defining passive righteousness both as imputation, and the change which occurs through Christ's indwelling. This is clear when he writes, "so far as justification is concerned, Christ and I must be so closely attached that He lives in me and I in Him."[109] He continues by stating that "Since Christ lives in me, grace, righteousness, life, and eternal salvation must be present with Him; and the Law, sin, and death must be absent."[110] Again, the transferring of Christ's righteousness is in terms of divine indwelling, rather than *extra*

106. Ibid.. 161.
107. Ibid., 164.
108. Ibid., 166.
109. Ibid., 167.
110. Ibid., 168.

*nos* imputation. This language would later be clarified by the Formula of Concord.

The life of the Christian is one that is lived in and through Christ. Luther summarizes Gal 2:20 by writing, "'Christ,' [Paul] says, 'is fixed and cemented to me and abides in me. The life that I now live, He lives in me. Indeed, Christ Himself is the life that I not live. In this way, therefore, Christ and I are one.'"[111] The life of active righteousness is not an autonomous enterprise, but is participation in the life of Christ himself. As in *On Christian Liberty*, Luther explains that in some sense the life of renovation is also due to alien righteousness. He writes, "Paul living in himself is utterly dead through the Law but living in Christ, or rather with Christ living in him, he lives an alien life. Christ is speaking, acting, and performing all actions in him; these belong not to the Paul-life, but to the Christ-life."[112] As is apparent elsewhere, Luther is not denying the fact that the Christian does actually perform good deeds and is himself renewed, but he gives the credit to Christ who lives within the Christian. This is essentially the *unio mystica*, or Christification. God himself dwells within and lives through the believer in order to renew him and help him to perform works of service for others. It is this which separates the active life of the Christian from that of the unbeliever. Luther expounds upon this essential distinction:

> Thus a Christian uses the world and all its creatures in such a way that there is no difference between him and an ungodly man. Their food and clothing are the same, their hearing and vision, and speaking are the same; their gestures, appearance, and shape are the same . . . Nevertheless there is the greatest possible difference. I do indeed live in the flesh, but I do not live on the basis of my own self. The life I now live in the flesh I live by faith in the Son of God. What you now hear me speak proceeds from another source than what you heard me speak before . . . For this [spiritual] life is in the heart through faith. There the flesh is extinguished; and there Christ rules with His Holy Spirit, who now sees, hears, speaks, works, suffers, and does simply everything in him, even though the flesh is still reluctant. In short, this life is not the life of the flesh, although it is a life in the flesh; but it is the life of Christ, the Son of God, whom the Christian possesses by faith.[113]

111. Ibid., 167.
112. Ibid., 170.
113. Ibid., 172.

In terms of outward obedience, there may not be any visible difference between the Christian and the righteous pagan. However, spiritually, the difference is immense. They do not differ simply in the fact that the believer has faith in Christ and the unbeliever does not, thus making the motivations different. Rather, they differ in that the living and acting of the Christian is the work of the Son and the Holy Spirit in and through him. The Christian and his Savior become "one flesh," as God works intimately in and through him in his renovation.

## Conclusion

The theme of the two kinds of righteousness is extensive within Luther's corpus. It is not simply an illustration used by the early Luther, nor is it a minor theme in his thought. The contemporary proponents of the two kinds of righteousness are perfectly in accord with Luther's own theology in utilizing this as a primary Lutheran distinctive. The distinction between active and passive righteousness begins in 1518 with Luther's sermons "Two Kinds of Righteousness" and "Threefold Righteousness." The distinction between active and passive righteousness in these two works roughly corresponds to the contemporary iterations of the threefold righteousness, especially in Biermann's work, but there are important differences. In these sermons, there is no clear division between imputation and Christ's life within the believer. Both justification and sanctification can in some sense be identified with passive righteousness. This would later be clarified by the Lutheran confessional documents. Luther does, however, seem more apt to distinguish these two realities in his later writings. Luther also does not explicitly utilize the distinction to differentiate between *coram mundo* and *coram Deo* relationships, though this may be a valid extrapolation from his teaching. At times, he does identify active righteousness almost exclusively as that which serves the neighbor. Also, Kolb's contention that Luther found the two kinds of righteousness to be "a true and accurate description of what it means to be human" is unfounded in Luther's writings on the subject.[114] He never utilizes this distinction to propound a specific anthropology, but to explain how humans relate to God and the broader world in which they live.[115]

---

114. Kolb, "Luther on Two Kinds," 464.

115. I am not convinced of Oswald Bayer's relational ontology, which stands behind Kolb's conviction here. Relation and being are not synonymous concepts. Kolb's

The discussion of Christ as favor and gift in *Against Latomus*, though not exactly parallel to the two kinds of righteousness, demonstrates Luther's concern to keep renewal and imputation separate. This distinction, perhaps more than what Luther calls the two kinds of righteousness, is essentially what the Formula of Concord proposes as the distinction between passive and active righteousness, or imputation and indwelling. In *The Freedom of the Christian*, Luther expounds upon Christian living in almost exclusively horizontal language. By faith, one receives Christ and his righteousness; by love, one serves the neighbor. Of all of the texts examined, this treatise comes closest to Kolb, Arand, and Biermann's proposal of active righteousness as a horizontal reality lived in the world. The 1535 Galatians commentary, as one of Luther's later works, demonstrates that the reformer's thinking did not change significantly on the topic of the two kinds of righteousness. He distinguishes between passive and active righteousness, between imputation and the good works of the Christian. Yet, even in this treatise, Luther does not always distinguish passive righteousness from divine indwelling.

The contemporary iterations of the two kinds of righteousness are largely consistent with Luther's thought. Its importance in Luther's writings demonstrates the usefulness of this teaching as a Lutheran distinctive. Rather than reducing all theological dialogue to an exposition of justification by faith, Luther emphasizes the necessity and importance of love toward the neighbor in the life of the Christian and the teaching of the church. There are, however, some important differentiations between Luther's view of the two kinds of righteousness and those explained by contemporary writers. First, Luther emphasizes union with Christ when explaining both passive and active righteousness. The marriage union of faith unites one to Christ's justifying righteousness; there is a corresponding indwelling of God in the Christian that corresponds to renewal and obedience to God's will. Second, Luther does not limit discussions of active righteousness to the second table of the law. This is an important emphasis in Luther, but he also encourages piety toward God as a vertical reality in response to God's act of deliverance in justification. Finally, Luther uses the two-kinds-of-righteousness distinction to explain the difference between faith and works in the Christian life, and not to explain any particular theological anthropology as do Kolb and Arand.

presuppositions regarding this connection allow him to view Luther's talk of relation as identification of who the human person is. However, I am convinced that Luther held to many of the metaphysical assumptions of his time. His revolution was a theological, not a philosophical, one. On Bayer's metaphysic, see his book *Theology the Lutheran Way*.

# The Two Kinds of Righteousness
# in the Lutheran Confessions

The teachings of the Lutheran Confessions are more essential to Lutheran identity than are the doctrines of Luther himself. Though the Lutheran tradition owes its origins to the work of the Wittenberg reformer, Lutheran theologians do not subscribe to the writings of Luther, but to the confessional documents written with the consent of the church. These are the writings compiled in the 1580 Book of Concord. When examining the various confessional documents, it is apparent that the distinction between the two kinds of righteousness is a valid explication of historic Lutheran teaching. The various documents compiled in the Book of Concord show a concern to demonstrate both that one's standing before God is a free gift of grace, and that one's active life in the world is guided by the law of God.

These following contentions explained in the beginning of this work will be demonstrated here from the confessional documents: The two kinds of righteousness is not a theological novelty, but is explained and defended within the foundational writings of the Lutheran church. The Lutheran tradition is, thus, not inherently antinomian or reductionistic; it is, in fact, the opposite. Good works and love are essential to Lutheran Confessional theology, though always subordinated to the centrality of justification by faith. These documents also demonstrate that the horizontal-vertical divide is not always strictly applied in Christian obedience, but that the Christian responds as an act of thanksgiving in love and piety toward God, alongside of horizontal love and good deeds performed for the sake of the neighbor. Finally, the Confessions do not explain the teaching of the two kinds of righteousness within the context of human identity, as do Kolb and Arand.

## Luther's Catechisms

Luther's doctrine of the two kinds of righteousness is not explicitly stated in his Small or Large Catechism. However, the two central realities which are inherent in this distinction, namely one's passive righteousness received from God, and one's active life in the world, are affirmed and expounded upon throughout. Through examining these texts, it becomes apparent that Luther speaks about the necessity of good works as guided by the Ten Commandments *coram mundo*, and the passive righteousness of faith *coram Deo*. The treatment of the Ten Commandments is the most important topic for the purposes of the present work. When examining the language of Luther in the catechisms, it will be apparent that these commands of God do not serve a purely negative function in his catechetical instruction, but also lay the framework by which the Christian is guided in the world before others.

In explaining the first commandment, Luther does not argue that its purpose is simply to demonstrate human inability. Rather, he applies this commandment to concrete situations in human life as a guiding norm for the believer.[1] Luther argues that the first commandment should be applied in terms of faith. He contends that "It is the trust and faith of the heart alone that make both God and an idol" (LC I.2). Under the papacy, Christians were urged to place their trust not simply in Christ, but in various saints. Similarly, pagan nations place their trust in false gods. In contrast to this, Luther contends, "We are to trust in God alone, to look to him alone, and to expect him to give us only good things" (LC I.24). This commandment urges Christians to give thanks for the things that God blesses us with. Parents should urge their own children to obey this commandment by teaching them both the threat and promise attached to it.[2] Obedience to this commandment is a *coram mundo* reality, as Luther explains that one must trust in God alone for all good gifts, so that "We walk straight ahead on the right path, using all of God's gifts exactly as a shoemaker uses

---

1. Edmund Schlink notes that "the new obedience of the regenerated is obedience to the same Ten Commandments through which God judges the sinner" (Schlink, *Theology*, 112).

2. "Consequently, in order to show that God will not have this commandment taken lightly but will strictly watch over it, he has attached to it, first, a terrible threat, and, then, a beautiful, comforting promise. Both of these should be thoroughly emphasized and impressed upon the young people so that they may take them to heart and remember them" (LC I .9).

a needle, awl, and thread for his work and afterwards puts them aside" (LC I.47). This is true of all people, who are called to "do the same in his or her walk of life according to God's order, allowing none of these things to be a lord or an idol" (LC I.48).[3] Luther applies this first commandment to one's vocation, so that it serves to guide one in serving the neighbor by acknowledging one's passive relationship before God in receiving his gifts, and thus motivates one to use these gifts rightly.[4]

Luther's explication of the second commandment similarly demonstrates that he expects people to look to the commandments for guidance in Christian living. He urges parents to train their children to obey God's commands: "Above all else, therefore, our young people should be strictly required and trained to hold this as well as the other commandments in high regard" (LC I.61). Luther is not simply stating that children need to know this commandment so that they might see their shortcomings and believe the gospel. He urges parents to punish their children when they break God's commands, so that they might learn to obey them. He writes, "Whenever they violate them, we must be after them at once with the rod, confront them with the commandment, and continually impress it upon them, so that they may be brought up not merely with punishment but with reverence and fear of God" (LC I.61).[5] Luther is not opposed to the idea of habituation. Along with urging parents to train their children to obey the commandments, he also speaks of habits that Christians should practice, such as commending oneself to God each morning and evening.

---

3. Schlink notes this connection: "God is feared and loved only in concrete obedience to his concrete commandments. God is loved only in love to the neighbor, as the second table concretely defines that love" (Schlink, *Theology*, 112).

4. There is an intimate connection here between one's faith vertically and the service of one's neighbor in the horizontal realm. Kolb notes, "Human life is cruciform—eyes lifted to focus on God, feet firmly planted on his earth, arms stretched out in mutual support of those God has placed around us" (Kolb, "Luther on Two Kinds of Righteousness," 456).

5. He writes similarly, later in the same section, "See, with simple and playful methods like this we should bring up young people in the fear and honor of God so that the First and Second Commandments may become familiar and constantly be practiced. Then some good may take root, spring up, and bear fruit, and people may grow to adulthood who may give joy and pleasure to an entire country. That would also be the right way to bring up children, while they may be trained with kind and agreeable methods. For what a person enforces by means of beatings and blows will come to no good end. At best, the children will remain good only as long as the rod is on their backs. But this kind of training takes root in their hearts so that they fear God more than they do rods and clubs" (LC I.75-77).

The second commandment, as the first, is something which the Christian is called to obey in view of the forgiveness of sins.

Throughout the rest of the catechism, there are several other statements of Luther which make it apparent that he intended his explanation of the Ten Commandments to be a guide for Christian life in the world. In explaining the fourth commandment, Luther speaks about the duties of children in relation to their parents: "For God's sake, therefore, let us finally learn that the young people should banish all other things from their sight and give first place to this commandment" (LC I.115). Luther expects that the youth should actually be able to do this in relation to their *coram mundo* relationship with their parents and elders. They are called to do this, not to earn favor with God, but because they "wish to serve God with truly good works" (LC I.115). When children do obey this commandment, they can say joyfully, "See, this work is well-pleasing to my God in heaven; this I know for certain" (ibid.). In contrast to the false good works encouraged by the Roman Church, the Ten Commandments allow Christians to have the joy of knowing that they are obeying God's commands, and are thus pleasing him in their actions.

Luther does not expound upon the Ten Commandments as a burden when viewed from the perspective of faith (i.e., the perspective of one whose imperfections are covered by the righteousness of Christ). Instead, Luther writes that "You should rejoice from the bottom of your heart and give thanks to God that he has chosen and made you worthy to perform works so precious and pleasing to him" (LC I.117). Though Christians should never boast in their work, the heart should "leap and overflow with joy" when one sees that one is performing works which God has commanded (LC I.120). Luther writes later, in a similar fashion, "Those who are obedient, willing and eager to be of service, and cheerfully do everything that honor demands, know that they please God and receive joy and happiness as their reward" (LC I.151). This further shows that the commandments, for Luther, are something which believers should delight in as they are guided in their lives.[6]

6. This has several implications for Christian preaching as well. Luther's Large Catechism itself is made up of a series of sermons, several of which are purely instruction in Christian living. Timothy Saleska explains, "Christians are responsible to live a life that reflects God's love to other humans and also to the rest of God's creation. God also assumes that Christians are to serve God according to His will and not their own. Therefore, Lutherans teach good works and how they are to be done. That means that part of the preacher's job is *to instruct* his people as to what the life of a Christian *tsaddik*

There is some discussion of the civil use of the law in Luther's Large Catechism. In speaking about the fifth commandment, which prohibits murder, he notes, "God wants to have everyone defended, delivered, and protected from the wickedness and violence of others, and he has placed this commandment as a wall, fortress, and refuge around our neighbors, so that no one may do them bodily harm or injury" (LC I.185). This commandment, in its strict and literal sense, is not given primarily for the sake of the church, but for the general order of society.[7] Luther mentions the civil use in the seventh commandment, condemning thieving, as well. He notes that this commandment is not to be preached primarily to Christians, but "chiefly to knaves and scoundrels, though it would certainly be more fitting if the judge, the jailer, or the hangman did the preaching" (LC I.232). The civic use of the law is essential in Luther's theology for restraining evil and promoting civil righteousness.

Luther summarizes the Ten Commandments in a third-use context. These commands are "a summary of divine teaching on what we are to do to make our whole life pleasing to God. They are the true fountain from which all good works must spring, the true channel from which all good works must flow" (LC I.311). These commandments are the standard of a good and God-pleasing life. These commandments also contain "a wrathful threat and a friendly promise, not only to terrify and warn us but also to attract and allure us, so that we will receive and regard God's Word as seriously as he does" (LC I.322). The commandments do not only condemn the sinner, but they even serve to entice one to obey them by the use of threats and promises. As children are taught the commandments, they may be brought up to obey them "in the fear and reverence of God" (LC I.330). Luther comments that the Old Testament had good reason to commend the people of Israel to keep God's law on their walls and garments. This encouraged the people of Israel to be obedient to God's commandments. Similarly, "Each of us is to make [the commandments] a matter of daily practice in all circumstances, in all activities and dealings, as if they were written everywhere we look, even wherever we go or wherever we stand," so that we might "find occasion to practice the Ten Commandments" (LC I.331–32). Luther holds to a strong doctrine of the third use of the law.

---

'looks like' and *to exhort* them to live as the righteous people God has called them to be" (Saleska, "Two Kinds," 142, emphasis in the original).

7. This is not to downplay the reality that this commandment also condemns man's universal struggle with anger, hatred, and bitterness toward others.

God's commandments are not purely condemnatory, but they give guidance to Christians in their horizontal life in this world.[8]

In a traditional law-gospel-reductionist schema, one would expect Luther to open his section on the Creed by commenting that in the Creed, sinners are shown the gospel of free grace which forgives transgression of God's law in the Ten Commandments. Luther does something rather different, however. He notes that the commandments tell us "all that God wishes us to do and not to do," and that the Creed then "sets forth all that we must expect and receive from God" (LC II.1). Luther does not set these two different words of God in opposition to one another, but instead he writes,

> [The Creed] is given in order to help us do what the Ten Commandments require of us. For as we said above, they are set so high that all human ability is far too puny and weak to keep them. Therefore it is just as necessary to learn this part as it is the other so that we may know where and how to obtain the power to do this. If we were able by our own strength to keep the Ten Commandments as they ought to be kept, we would need nothing else, neither the Creed nor the Lord's Prayer. (LC II.2–3)

The purpose of the Creed, for Luther, is not merely to forgive us for our failure to obey the law (forgiveness and imputed righteousness are not even mentioned in the introduction!), but rather, it gives us the power to begin to obey God's commandments. It is the gospel which gives one the power to begin to obey God's law, because the law cannot grant the ability to perform what it commands.

Growth in holiness is mentioned throughout the second part of the Large Catechism. Luther states that "holiness has begun and is growing daily," yet it is not yet complete in this life because "we are never without sin because we carry flesh around our neck" (LC II 57, 54). Active righteousness grows through two means: the Christian church and the forgiveness of sins. Thus passive righteousness (justification) grants growth in active righteousness (sanctification). Luther's concept of union is also apparent in his discussion of the Creed, wherein he mentions that "God gives himself completely to us," and this union with the Holy Trinity gives us the ability "to keep the Ten Commandments" (LC II.68–69). Another manner

---

8. "Good works are no longer only something demanded, nor only something imputed, but they become a reality as deeds of the believers themselves" (Schlink, *Theology*, 112).

in which Luther speaks of these two different kinds of righteousness is by speaking of the Creed as that which "brings pure grace and makes us righteous and acceptable to God," which then helps us to "love and delight in all the commandments of God" (LC II.69). It is clear that throughout the second part of the Large Catechism, the gospel presented in the Apostle's Creed is said to grant both the forgiveness of sins and the ability to begin to fulfill the commandments of God.

In introducing the Lord's Prayer, Luther mentions that perfect obedience to the Ten Commandments is impossible, even for the greatest Christian. Yet, he does not then simply point to the Lord's Prayer as a means by which the believer only asks for God's forgiveness, but writes, "Consequently, nothing is so necessary as to call upon God incessantly and to drum into his ears our prayer that he may give, preserve, and increase in us faith and the fulfillment of the Ten Commandments and remove all that stands in our way and hinders us in this regard" (LC III.2). Though Luther certainly emphasizes the forgiveness of sins on account of Christ in his treatment of the Lord's Prayer, he makes it a central purpose of the prayer that it helps God's people begin to be obedient to God's commandments.

The forgiveness of sins is emphasized especially in Luther's treatment of the two sacraments of baptism and the Lord's Supper. Regarding baptism, Luther states that "through it we become completely holy and blessed," referencing the complete and perfect holiness that the Christian obtains through Christ (LC IV.46). Similarly, Luther explains the purpose of the Supper by saying, "For this reason he bids me to eat and drink, that it may be mine and do me good as a sure pledge and sign—indeed, as the very gift he has provided for me against my sins, death, and all evils" (LC V.22). Luther does not, however, limit the sacraments solely to instruments of passive righteousness. Here, he also mentions the importance of the reality of the active righteousness of the Christian. He argues that through the drowning of the Old Adam in baptism, "this corruption must daily decrease so that the longer we live the more gentle, patient, and meek we become, and the more we break away from greed, hatred, envy, and pride" (LC IV.67). Baptism grants both the forgiveness of sins and the destruction of the sin nature, because through the sacrament "the old creature daily decreases until finally destroyed" (LC IV.71). While Luther's treatment of the Sacrament of the Altar is mostly focused on passive righteousness, he mentions that "The Lord's Supper is given as a daily food and sustenance so that our faith may be refreshed and strengthened and that it may not succumb in the struggle but become stronger and stronger" (LC V 24). The life imparted in the sacraments "should be one that continually develops and progresses" (LC V 25). The sacraments grant both the favor of God and the *donum*, so that the Christian is forgiven and strengthened unto obedience.

The three kinds of righteousness are apparent throughout Luther's Large Catechism. Though Luther begins by discussing the law, and then the gospel, a reductionistic law-gospel schema does not exactly fit the particular structure of his writing. Luther places the Ten Commandments in the context of one who is saved and desires to be obedient to God's law, which is why Luther gives practical instruction especially for parents to teach the commands to their children. He then presents the gospel in the form of the Creed, not simply as the answer to one's inability to fulfill the law, but also as that which gives the power to obey the Ten Commandments. Similarly, Luther's treatments of the Lord's Prayer and the sacraments emphasize both the reality of the forgiveness of sins and the ability God grants for one to grow in the life of faith and obey God's commandments. There is a clear third use of the law in Luther's catechism, and that use is primarily a horizontal reality, as Luther explains even the first two commandments in a way which serves the neighbor in one's vocation. It is also clear that justification and the life of obedience are connected realities, but clearly distinguished. One's salvation is received solely by faith in the message of the Creed, but the Christian's life in the world consists in his obedience to God's commands. The two-kinds-of-righteousness paradigm is implicitly taught within the Large Catechism, and while passive righteousness is central, active righteousness is a necessity for the Christian; it includes obedience to both tables of the law.

## The Augsburg Confession

As a summary of the newly defined Lutheran faith, the Augsburg Confession gives the first concise and comprehensive statement about the relationship between faith and good works in a confessional document. There is no extensive discussion about the "two kinds of righteousness" explicitly here, but several articles do address justification, the role of good works, and the righteousness of the unbeliever. According to the Augsburg Confession, both faith (passive righteousness), and works (active righteousness) are necessary, each within its proper sphere.

Article IV of the Augsburg Confession addresses the topic of justification, arguing that "human beings cannot be justified before God by their own powers, merits, or works" (AC IV.1). Thus good works are excluded from justification *coram Deo*. Rather, human beings are "justified as a gift on account of Christ through faith when they believe that they are received into grace and that their sins are forgiven on account of Christ, who by his death made satisfaction for our sins. God reckons this faith as righteousness" (AC VI.2–3). Justification is received through faith alone, because of the work of Christ—especially through his vicarious death.

The Augsburg Confession discusses the nature of good works particularly in two different sections: Article VI, on new obedience, and Article XX, on good works. Article VI states that faith "is bound to yield good fruits," but that these fruits are never the cause of one's justification (AC VI.1–2). These good works are to be performed "on account of God's will" (AC VI.1). Article XII, on repentance, echoes this teaching by stating that good works, as the "fruit of repentance," always follow contrition and faith (AC XII.6). This is expounded upon in Article XX, regarding faith and good works. In this section, the confessors defend their faith against the contention that they prohibited and rejected good works due to their emphasis on justifying faith. There are three primary contentions made here by the writers of the Augsburg Confession. First, justification does not arise through good works: "It is only by faith that forgiveness of sins and grace are apprehended" (AC XX.28). In contrast to the works-righteousness of the medieval church, the reformers had to emphasize the centrality of faith so that the gospel might be clearly proclaimed. Second, faith must be taught prior to good works, because it is only through faith that truly good works can arise. The Augsburg Confession states that "because the Holy Spirit is received trough faith, consequently hearts are renewed and endowed with new affections so as to be able to do good works" (AC XX.29). The reformers did not reject good works, but argued that faith must be present prior to good works. Third, the reformers argue that it is Rome that does not teach good works, because they have instead rejected the commandments of God for human traditions. The writers of the Augsburg Confession argue that the preachers in Rome "urged childish and needless works, such as particular holy days and fasts, brotherhoods, pilgrimages, the cult of the saints, rosaries, monasticism, and the like" (AC XX.3). According to the Augsburg

Confession, good works are truly necessary, but arise only through the Spirit's work in justification.[9]

Article VIII mentions the nature of free will, and in doing so distinguishes between the civil righteousness of the unbeliever and the actual righteousness of the Christian. Apart from the regenerating action of the Holy Spirit, the human creature does have some capacity to act freely. This is true regarding "civil righteousness and for choosing things subject to reason" (AC XVIII.1). This is the first kind of righteousness, or civic righteousness. The Augsburg Confession then argues that unregenerate free will "does not have the power to produce the righteousness of God or spiritual righteousness without the Holy Spirit" (AC XVIII.2). Though unbelievers perform externally good works which benefit society and function according to reason, they cannot perform truly good actions which proceed from faith. The third kind of righteousness, that which is truly good, is "worked in the heart when the Holy Spirit is received through the Word" (AC XVIII.3). The differentiating factor in terms of the active righteousness between the unbeliever and the believer is the Holy Spirit. This distinction is also noted in Article XX, which speaks about the philosophers who "tried to live honestly" but were incapable of doing so because they lacked both faith and the Holy Spirit (AC XX.33–34).

The Augsburg Confession teaches three clear realities about human righteousness. First, one's justification is received solely by faith. This is a passive reality wherein the Christian receives Christ's perfect righteousness apart from any works whatsoever. Second, justifying faith always produces good works. They are not optional for the Christian, but are to be performed because it is God's will that one do so. Third, there is a kind of righteousness that unbelievers can perform, but this is a civil righteousness based upon reason. It is not true righteousness because it is not accompanied by faith and the Holy Spirit. The three-kinds-of-righteousness paradigm explicated by Biermann is thus implicitly taught in the Augsburg Confession.

9. There is an intimate connection between justification and active righteousness. Arand and Biermann write, "Luther stressed that the passive righteousness of faith does not remain relevant only for realities in heaven; it belongs also to earthly realities and contributes to the pursuit of active righteousness within the world" (Arand, "Why the Two Kinds," 122).

## The Apology of the Augsburg Confession

In his Apology of the Augsburg Confession, Philip Melanchthon speaks extensively about two different kinds of righteousness in Article IV, on justification. He posits that the two kinds of righteousness correspond to philosophical righteousness and justifying righteousness. While Luther utilizes this distinction primarily to explain the difference between justification and sanctification, Melanchthon uses twofold-righteousness terminology primarily in reference to the distinction between passive and civil righteousness. There are several other statements in the document which do demonstrate, however, that Melanchthon is also concerned with distinguishing between the active righteousness of the Christian and of the unregenerate person. Thus, as in the Augsburg Confession, Melanchthon speaks of a threefold righteousness, and does so in explicit terms.

Melanchthon argues that there are two different kinds of righteousness within the Decalogue itself. First, it requires "outward civil works," which can, to an extent, be produced by reason alone (Apol. IV.8); and second, it requires much beyond mere external righteousness, instructing the believer "truly to fear God, truly to love God, truly to call upon God, truly to be convinced that he hears us, and to expect help from God in death and affliction" (Apol. IV.8). These outward civil works are performed by both believers and unbelievers, because God-given reason can produce such deeds. The other good works, namely the first table, are given to Christians, because only by faith can one begin to be obedient to God's commandments.

The righteousness of reason is a divine gift. Melanchthon does not reject the righteousness of reason or seek to minimize its usefulness within the world. Reason promotes works which are for "society's welfare" (Apol. IV.18) and which can even earn temporal rewards (Apol. IV.24). These works can be performed "to some extent without Christ and without the Holy Spirit" (Apol. IV.130). In this context, Melanchthon even promotes the use of pagan ethicists such as Aristotle (Apol. IV.14). The scholastic theologians were not wrong to use Aristotle, or to engage in ethical discourse. The error which Melanchthon is seeking to correct is a confusion of civil righteousness and proper Christian righteousness. Biermann notes that "Melanchthon's quarrel was not so much with Aristotle, as with his opponents' inappropriate use of Aristotle . . . Aristotle was not the problem; it was the imposition of Aristotle into a question of theology *coram Deo* that brought Melanchthon's rebuke."[10] He further demonstrates that "not only did he use Aristotelian method, but Melanchthon openly endorsed the philosopher, finding opportunities explicitly to praise Aristotle's contributions even while confessing the Lutheran faith."[11] Aristotle is good and helpful in his own particular sphere, but if he is used beyond that sphere, theology and philosophy are conflated.[12]

The late medieval scholastic theologians, according to Melanchthon, were guilty of conflating active and passive righteousness. He asks, "if [philosophical righteousness] is Christian righteousness, what is the difference between philosophy and the teaching of Christ? If we merit the forgiveness of sins by these elicited acts of ours, what does Christ provide?" (Apol. IV.12). Theology and philosophy are both necessary disciplines, but they need to be exercised within their proper spheres. The scholastics, by arguing that one was justified by philosophic righteousness, left no place for the work of Christ in justification. In doing this, the scholastic theologians committed the same error as the Pharisees. They "teach nothing but the righteousness of reason or at the very least, the righteousness of the law, upon which they fasten their attention just as the Jews did upon the veiled face of Moses" (Apol. IV.21). Melanchthon does not seek to denigrate the usefulness of the law, nor the righteousness of reason, which deserves great praise (Apol. IV.24); instead he argues for the negation of reason and works in justification.

Though reason itself does useful works, there is an immense difference between the good works of the regenerate and unregenerate person. Melanchthon asserts that "without the Holy Spirit the human heart either despises the judgment of God in its complacency or in the face of punishment flees and hates God who judges them" (Apol. IV.34). While external obedience to parts of the second table of the law is possible through reason alone, the unregenerate heart does not fear, love, and trust in God. Without faith, fulfillment of the law is impossible. The believer, however, through repentance is regenerated and "able to live according to the law of God, namely, to love God, truly to fear God, truly to assert that God hears prayer, to obey God in all afflictions, and to mortify concupiscence, etc."

10. Biermann, *Case for Character*, 84–85.

11. Ibid., 83.

12. Biermann notes that Aristotle was embraced by both Luther and Melanchthon as a helpful guide in civic ethical matters, which he argues is a tie between Lutheran ethics and twentieth-century virtue ethics (ibid., 85).

(Apol. IV.45). The confusion of the two kinds of righteousness is not only the conflation of justification and civic righteousness, but also of inchoate Christian righteousness and philosophic righteousness. Melanchthon draws a sharp line of distinction between the righteousness of the pagan and the Christian; the unregenerate person is not able to follow God's law, whereas the regenerate person is.

Faith necessarily produces good works within the believer. Through faith, one receives not only the forgiveness of sins, but also spiritual life.[13] Faith necessarily brings forth good fruit within the Christian, and one cannot simultaneously have faith and commit mortal sin (Apol. IV.64). At this point in the Reformation the strict divide between justification as forensic and regeneration as effective had not been made. Melanchthon argues that the term "justification" can refer either to the fact that "out of unrighteous people righteous people are made or regenerated" or "that they are pronounced or regarded as righteous" (Apol. IV.72). It is in this way that Melanchthon argues that good works are not a cause, but an effect, of justification. Faith receives God's promise in the gospel, and then performs good works for the neighbor.

Throughout the Apology, Melanchthon expresses his conviction that the ordinary nature of the Christian life is one of growth and progress. The Holy Spirit creates new impulses in the heart of the believer, which begins a process whereby the Christian begins to fulfill the law of God. Melanchthon writes that "we ought to keep the law and then keep it more and more" (Apol. IV.124). After justification, the Christian begins to trust in God and love the neighbor. These works are impossible apart from the Holy Spirit and are thus not attributable to civic righteousness. When the Holy Spirit is received, God's law "can be kept" (Apol. IV.132). This keeping of the law "must begin in us and then increase more and more" (Apol. IV.136). Melanchthon is quick to clarify that although sanctification is a reality, one will never arrive at a state of perfection in this life. He confesses that "we are a long way from the perfect keeping of the law" (Apol. IV.175). One's standing *coram Deo* is *always* based upon faith, because even the most sanctified Christian fails to be perfectly obedient and thus cannot trust in his own merit in regards to justification. Christian growth is progressive, but that growth is grounded upon justification.

---

13. "This faith, which arises and consoles in the midst of those fears, receives the forgiveness of sins, justifies us, and makes alive. For this consolation is a new and spiritual life" (Apol. IV.62).

The Apology contains Luther's distinction between passive and active righteousness. In the text, Melanchthon argues that the primary problem with medieval scholasticism is the confusion of civic and justifying righteousness. Thus, most often, he speaks of active righteousness in reference to Aristotelian ethics. However, Melanchthon also is intent on distinguishing between civic righteousness and the active righteousness of the Christian. The primary differentiating factors are the faith of the one performing the actions and the indwelling Holy Spirit. The works of unbelievers are done by reason and do not fulfill the first table of the law. It is only the regenerate who can begin to fulfill God's law in the world. They do so through faith which justifies. There is a process whereby the believer is made progressively more obedient to God's will, though this never results in perfect obedience. Melanchthon's argument roughly corresponds to the three kinds of righteousness promoted by Biermann, but he does not make the strict vertical/horizontal dichotomy as found in contemporary proponents of the two kinds of righteousness, and in some of Luther's writings. He often equates active righteousness with Godward works, such as trust, love, and fear of God, rather than horizontal actions performed for the good of the neighbor. This is where the category of eucharistic sacrifice must be placed into the horizontal/vertical dynamic, so that love and praise of God has a proper place within one's theological system. There is also, once again, no utilization of the two-kinds-of-righteousness distinction in the context of any type of relational ontology. Rather, Melanchthon assumes a rather traditional Greek metaphysic and discusses twofold righteousness simply as a means to distinguish faith and works.

## The Formula of Concord

Many of the prominent debates within the Lutheran church following Luther's death centered on the relationship between faith and works. Several articles in the Formula of Concord expound upon the righteousness that justifies and the good works of the Christian in the world. When examining the text, it becomes evident that the concept of the two kinds of righteousness is utilized by the second-generation reformers, just as it was by Luther and Melanchthon. The Formula is concerned not only with justification, but with a proper approach to Christian ethics and love. The language of twofold righteousness is used to distinguish divine imputation from the indwelling of the Holy Trinity, thus demonstrating the connection between the indwelling of Christ and the believer's active righteousness. The differences between the reformers and some contemporary iterations of the two kinds of righteousness are also once again apparent. The Formula does not limit active righteousness to the horizontal sphere, and it also does not utilize the concept as a means of explaining the human essence.

## The Osiandrian Dispute

Article III of the Formula of Concord is written concerning the theology of Andreas Osiander. Osiander was a student of Luther who sought to remain consistent with his teacher's thought throughout his career. He argued that the righteousness that justifies is Christ's essential divinity which indwells the Christian. In doing so, Osiander denied the forensic nature of justification, the necessary connection between both of Christ's natures, and the centrality of the works of redemption in history. In contradistinction to Osiander, the authors of the Formula contend:

> Christ is our righteousness not only according to his divine nature and also not only according to his human nature, but according to both natures. As God and as human being he has redeemed us from all sin, made us righteous, and saved us through his perfect obedience. Therefore, they [the reformers] have taught that the righteousness of faith is the forgiveness of sins, reconciliation with God, and that we are accepted as children of God for the sake of Christ's obedience alone, which is reckoned as righteousness through faith alone, out of sheer grace, to all who truly believe. Because of this, they are absolved from their unrighteousness. (FC SD III.4)

The reformers contended that justification is a forensic act based upon the active and passive obedience of Christ. Passive righteousness must not be conflated with any change that occurs within the believer.

In this context, the Formula contends that believers must necessarily perform good works. The gratuity of justification does not mean "that we should pursue sinning or remain and continue in sin without repentance, conversion, and improvement" (FC SD III.22). Those who are justified have received the Holy Spirit, through whom love toward both God and neighbor is created (FC SD III.23). Those who do not demonstrate good works and do not genuinely love others "are not justified but rather are still in death or have lost the righteousness of faith" (FC SD III.27). The Christian's sanctification, or renewal, is a divine gift worked by the Holy Spirit, just as faith and justification are (FC SD III.28). The Formula of Concord is not "weak on sanctification,"[14] but professes its truthfulness and importance boldly. However, the importance of both justification and renewal should not then serve as grounds for conflating the two acts of God. One must "not introduce into the article of justification itself or . . . mix with it what precedes faith or what results from it, as if they were necessary parts of it and belonged to it" (FC SD III.24). It is in this context that the Formula of Concord uses explicit "two kinds of righteousness" terminology. The text states:

> It is correct to say that in this life believers who have become righteous through faith in Christ have first of all the righteousness of faith that is reckoned to them and then thereafter the righteousness of new obedience or good works that are begun in them. But *these two kinds of righteousness* dare not be mixed with each other or simultaneously introduced into the article on justification by faith before God. For because this righteousness that is begun in us—this renewal—is imperfect and impure in this life because of our flesh, a person cannot use it in any way to stand before God's judgment throne. Instead, only the righteousness of the obedience, suffering, and death of Christ, which is reckoned to faith, can stand before God's tribunal. Even following their renewal, when they already are producing many good works and living the best kind of life, human beings please God, are acceptable to him, and receive adoption as children and heirs of eternal life only because of Christ's obedience. (FC SD III.32, emphasis mine)

The authors of the Formula did not reject Osiander's views regarding the indwelling of Christ's divinity completely. Osiander's flaw was not that he argued that God indwells the Christian, or that the believer is gradually conformed to the image of Christ. This is confessed when the Formula contends that "God the Father, Son, and Holy Spirit, who is the eternal and essential righteousness, dwells in the elect . . . For all Christians are temples of the Father, Son, and Holy Spirit, who moves them to act properly" (FC SD III.54). Yet this divine indwelling which changes the regenerate person "is not the righteousness of faith" (ibid.). In contradistinction to the Formula, Osiander conflated what must always be kept distinct. Justification and renewal must not be confused.

14. This is a slogan that appears on some popular Lutheran merchandise.

The reformers contend that believers "have the beginnings of renewal, sanctification, love, virtues, and good works," but that this refers to the second kind of righteousness, and these blessings cannot be confused with justification *sola fide* in one's relationship to God (FC SD III.35). The authors give two specific reasons why these two kinds of righteousness must be distinguished: First, arguing that one's standing before God is in any sense based on a change within the Christian takes away from the dignity of Christ and his redemptive work. Second, it gives no hope to burdened consciences. Only Christ, not any level of sanctification, can serve as a grounds for assurance.[15] Though good works are essential and beneficial, they are not part of our "righteousness before God" (FC SD III.39). This particular terminology is notable, because good works are said to be righteousness, but not righteousness *before God (coram Deo)*. There is an implicit distinction between vertical and horizontal righteousness in this article, though active righteousness also has a vertical element.

## The Controversy over Good Works

Another debate arose during the Reformation over the nature of good works, surrounding two particularly problematic phrases. George Major, a celebrated theologian and pastor, argued that good works are necessary for salvation. Borrowing from Melanchthon, Major was not intending to propose that such works were necessary for justification, but "Major defined the German word *Seligkeit* [salvation] as the result of justification, the whole experience of being saved."[16] Thus, Major simply was attempting to explicate the necessity of good works in the Christian life. However, due to Major's over-extensive use of the term "salvation," which was utilized most often in reference to justification, he was viewed as a compromiser. Niko-

15. Arand and Biermann explain: "The need to distinguish the two kind of righteousness necessitates that our active righteousness dare never become the basis for our righteousness *coram Deo*. For any attempt to bring works into the presence of God will lead to a rejection of the Creator-creature relationship whereby we receive our identity and life as children of God as a sheer gift. And so the Reformation teaching argued that standing before God in heaven, human beings must leave all works behind on earth and seek nothing but the righteousness of Christ that is received by faith. When terrors of conscience result from the recognition of one's inability to obtain salvation (Rome) or inability to find assurance of salvation (Pietism), it becomes dramatically obvious that active righteousness must remain on earth within the realm of our relationships with our fellow human creatures" (Arand and Biermann, "Why the Two Kinds," 121).

16. Arand, *Lutheran Confessions*, 191.

laus von Amsdorf, a friend of Major, vehemently opposed the utilization of such terminology, as he argued that salvation and justification are synonyms. In a tract published in 1557, Amsdorf contended, in contradistinction to Major, that good works are "detrimental to salvation," thus bringing the charge of antinomianism on himself.

Both of these figures represented extreme views on the subject of faith and works, though it is perhaps true that "the two and those who took their respective sides talked past each other."[17] Both figures defined the term "salvation" differently, which resulted in misunderstanding. Major assumed that Amsdorf taught that good works were unnecessary in the Christian life, and Amsdorf believed Major to be putting good works in the realm of justification. Throughout his life, Major defended his belief in *sola fide*, and Amsdorf insisted that the phrase "good works are detrimental to salvation" was only in reference to trust in one's good works, and did not deny their necessity or importance in the Christian life. Eventually, Major would recant his views and even deny having ever held to them, while Amsdorf continued to use problematic phrasing.[18] Despite the fact that the controversy was largely due to phraseology, there were some distinctive differences between the two positions. Though Major held firmly to his belief in *sola fide*, he argued that good works are salvific in two senses. First, they are necessary, not for initial justification, but for entrance into eschatological life, not as meritorious causes, but as an obligation for Christians. Second, Major proposed that "good works are necessary for the retention of salvation."[19] Both figures, though perhaps not as extreme as the isolated problematic phrases may imply, demonstrated two different sides within the debate over the relationship between faith and works in early Lutheranism.

The fourth article of the Formula of Concord sought to answer the questions related to Major and Amsdorf by setting forth a discussion of good works which avoids the errors of both antinomianism and legalism. The Formula outlines several areas of concord, thus demonstrating that there was significant agreement between both parties involved in this particular debate. First, both sides contended that believers should do good works, and that those good works are a result of the Spirit's work within

17. Ibid.

18. "In 1555 he protested to King Christian of Denmark that he had never taught that good works are necessary to salvation, nor did he at that time, nor would he ever in the future" (ibid., 193).

19. Ibid., 192.

the Christian, rather than a product of innate human powers. Second, good works are only accepted as good before God due to the merit of Christ, which covers human sin.[20]

Antinomianism is condemned throughout Article IV of the Formula. The reformers argue that though the phrase "good works are necessary *for salvation*" (emphasis mine) is unhelpful, good works are necessary in the Christian life. They write that "Holy Scripture itself uses words like 'necessity,' 'necessary,' and 'necessarily' and 'should' and 'must' to describe what we are bound to do according to God's order, command, and will'" (FC SD IV.14). David Scaer notes that "Intolerable was the view that the Christian, who knew of his justification by faith without works, would entertain the thought of leading an immoral life without paying proper attention to the Law and to good works. The preacher of the Gospel has the obligation of urging his flock in the performance of good works."[21] Good works are not optional in the Christian's life, and no one who is truly justified can live a life without good works. There is a "dead or illusory faith" which exists without good works, and this faith cannot save (FC SD IV.15). The writers condemn the idea that "true faith and the evil intention to remain and continue in sin could exit in a single heart at the same time! That is impossible" (FC SD IV.15). They also argue that Christians cannot retain faith and salvation if they would "remain in sin against their conscience or intentionally give themselves over to sin" (FC SD IV.15). Good works are necessary in that it is God's will that the Christian should do them, and the Christian therefore *must* perform them. True faith results in good works.[22] The authors of the Formula condemn, therefore, the contention that "good works are a matter of freedom for the faithful, in the sense that they have free choice whether they want or wish to do them or refrain from doing them or even to act against God's law while nevertheless still retaining faith, God's favor, and grace" (FC SD IV.20). Every form of antinomianism is rejected.

Along with condemning antinomianism, the Confessions argue that good works have no place in one's salvation, in contradistinction to Major's claim. The Formula states that "it is proper to reject the *propositiones* that good works are necessary for the salvation of believers or that it is impossible to be saved without good works" (FC SD IV.22). This phraseology is

20. These points are made in FC SD IV.6–8.

21. Scaer, "Good Works," in Preus, *Contemporary Look*, 165.

22. David Scaer rightly says, "Faith never exists without good works. In every instance faith by its inner nature produces good works" (ibid.).

dangerous because it seems to contradict Paul's contention that salvation is received by faith alone. Even if these phrases can be understood in an orthodox manner, they are unhelpful as they can "deprive troubled, distressed consciences of the comfort of the gospel" and "give them reason to doubt" (FC SD IV.23).[23] They also might cause one to become boastful in one's own good works, thinking that they are an aspect of one's salvation. In short, "In the discussion of the justification of the sinner before God, works and the role they play have no part whatsoever."[24] The Formula denies that good works have a bearing on one's *coram Deo* relationship. Although living a life devoid of good works in unrepentant sin can destroy salvation, grace can never be merited or preserved by good deeds. Passive righteousness is full and free, and must not be confused with sanctification. David Scaer writes, "In the relationship between God and man, God and not man does good works. Good works have their place in the relationship of one person to another but not in the relationship of God to man."[25] To use the phrase "good works are necessary for salvation" is to confuse active and passive righteousness by placing active righteousness within the realm of God's saving alien righteousness.

The debate surrounding good works was not only about one's initial justification, or simple nuances of a particular phraseology; it also surrounded the role of good works within the justified Christian's life. The Formula argues that salvation can be lost in the Christian life if one lives without repentance, seeking to abuse grace as an excuse to live in sin. On the other hand, however, one cannot and should not then conclude that good works are necessary for the maintenance or furthering of salvation. One's *coram Deo* relationship does not simply begin by faith, then allow itself to be guided by works. Rather, the Apostle Paul "attributes everything—the beginning, middle, and end—to faith alone" (FC SD IV.34). The status one has before God is *always* and *only* established by faith. While

---

23. "Works set within the context of the sinner's justification before God were regarded as personally damaging to the sinner. The Christian, believing that his justification depends on the work he performs, directs his faith away from Christ and toward his own works. He thus deprives himself of the comfort of Christ's work and is driven to despair, or he begins trusting in his own righteousness. In either case he eventually loses the hope of his salvation. Even with a mitigating explanation, the phrase 'good works are necessary for salvation' should never be used. No explanations can really remove the damage inflicted by misunderstandings" (ibid, 168).

24. Ibid., 166.

25. Ibid., 167.

sin can eradicate faith, good works cannot retain or improve faith. This confession guards against antinomianism, in contending that one can fall away from grace without repentance, and against works righteousness, by arguing that faith is not preserved or increased by one's good deeds.

The distinction between the "two kinds of righteousness" is essentially an explication of the reformers' position between the perceived antinomianism of Amsdorf and the works-righteousness of Major. It allows one to speak boldly of the necessity and importance of good works in the Christian life, as well as in preaching,[26] while also guarding against problematic phrasing such as "good works are necessary for salvation." *Coram Deo*, good works cannot and must not have any place. Justification is a full and free gift where works do not matter at all. However, *coram mundo*, works are an absolute necessity, and the Christian must be obedient to God, as faith shows itself through love.

## The Antinomian Controversy

While Luther's early writing emphasized one's relationship *coram Deo* by faith alone in contrast to the legalism inherent in the medieval church, his later writings emphasize the nature and importance of good works. One of Luther's friends and students, John Agricola, published an anonymous series of theses wherein he argued that the law does not need to be preached to Christians.[27] According to Agricola, the law is to be proclaimed only in the civil sphere, and should not be taught in the church. It is the gospel which brings one to repentance and faith, and the gospel alone should guide preaching. Because of Agricola's views on law and gospel, Luther ceased supporting the other reformer's writings. Agricola responded by arguing that Luther was inconsistent with his own position on justification; Agricola purported that according to Luther, that there are two separate justifications: one by faith, and one by works. Eventually Luther wrote a series of theses against those who he labeled "antinomians" in 1537. This last controversy of Luther's life consisted of four separate disputations against those who held to Agricola's position, though Agricola himself recanted his views in 1541 (just five years before Luther's death).

---

26. "Christians should not be restrained from good works but admonished and urged most diligently to do them" (FC SD IV.40).

27. The historical information here is taken from the historical introduction to Luther, *Only the Decalogue*, 11–21.

The fifth and sixth articles of the Formula of Concord were written in response to the antinomian position on law and gospel. In Article V, the reformers argue against both Agricola's position that the law is irrelevant to the life of the church, and Philip Melanchthon's definition of the gospel which included commands within it.[28] Henry Hamman writes, "The view that good works are necessary for salvation (see Article IV), which arose among Melanchthon's followers, seemed to correspond with the unclear presentation of Law and Gospel and their respective effects that was regarded as a mark of the school of Melanchthon."[29] Though Melanchthon himself did not seek to compromise the doctrine of justification, some of his statements about the gospel led others to improperly distinguish between law and gospel. It is in contrast to both Agricola's antinomianism and Melanchthon's confusing language about the gospel that Article V was written on the necessity of distinguishing law from gospel.

Article VI is written with the same controversy in mind, dealing not with the distinction between the law and the gospel *per se*, but about the continuing validity of God's law in the life of the Christian. Andreus Musculus, a theologian from Brandenburg, contended for a modified form of Agricola's antinomianism.[30] Though acknowledging that the law has validity for the Christian life, especially in convicting one of sin, Musculus was skeptical of Melanchthon's statements about a third use of the law. In contrast to Melanchthon, Musculus argued that good works are spontaneous rather than coerced, and that therefore the Christian has no need of God's law to serve as a guide or instructor. In opposition to this, the authors of the Formula of Concord contended that Melanchthon's division between three uses of the law is valid, and that God's law continues to serve as a guide for the Christian in a life of God-pleasing works.

Even though Christians are freed from the curse of the law, they still "should daily practice the law of the Lord" (FC SD VI.4). God's law is necessary for the Christian throughout his life. The reformers contend:

28. "A dispute occurred in this regard among some theologians of the Augsburg Confession. One party held that the gospel is really not only the proclamation of grace but also at the same time a proclamation of repentance, which reproves the greatest sin, unbelief" (FC SD V.2).

29. Hamann, "Law and Gospel," in Preus, *Contemporary Look*, 174.

30. A brief history of this controversy may be found in Arand, *Lutheran Confessions*, 198–99.

> Although those who believe in Christ are truly motivated by the
> Spirit of God and do the will of God according to their inward per-
> son from a free spirit, nevertheless the Holy Spirit uses the written
> law on them to teach them, so that through it believers in Christ
> learn to serve God not according to their own ideas but according
> to his written law and Word, which is a certain rule and guiding
> principle for directing the godly life and behavior according to the
> eternal and unchanging will of God. (FC SD VI.2–3)

Musculus was correct that believers freely perform good works due to their
renewal and the indwelling Spirit. However, if one were simply left to oneself, without an external word from God, one would likely begin creating
man-made laws to obey instead of those which God has directly given. The
law serves as a guide for the Christian, outlining exactly what works the
Christian ought to perform in obedience to God and in service to one's
neighbor. This law of God is "a mirror that accurately depicts the will of
God and what pleases him. It should always be held before the faithful and
taught among them continuously and diligently" (FC SD VI.4). The Formula cites Psalm 119 as an example of how Christians should continue to
look to God's law for guidance and delight.

The law does not purely serve as a guide for the Christian. It also has
several other functions. Because Christians still have the flesh clinging to
them, "they also need [the law's] punishments, so that they may be incited
by them and follow God's Spirit" (FC SD VI.9). The law should be used to
beat one's flesh and keep one's sinful nature obedient to the will of God.
Due to their sinful nature, Christians are "lazy, indolent, and recalcitrant,"
and God's law serves to reprove them (FC SD VI.12). The sinful aspect of
human nature must be "forced into obedience" by the law, including by its
threats and punishments (FC SD VI.24). The external law is only necessary because Christians are imperfectly renewed. The Formula states that
in heaven, Christians "will need neither the proclamation of the law nor its
threats and punishment" (FC SD VI.24). This does not mean, however, that
the law itself is only temporal. It is the external *recitation* of the law which
is temporal. This is clear in that the Formula refers to God's law as "the
unchanging will of God" (FC SD VI.15), and "the eternal and unchanging
will of God" (FC SD VI.3). When the flesh is stripped away, the law will be
fulfilled, not by coercion, but "by the power of the indwelling Spirit of God
spontaneously, without coercion, unhindered, perfectly and completely,
with sheer joy, and they will delight in his will eternally" (FC SD VI.25).

The law itself is unchanging and eternal; it is merely the motivation and extent of one's obedience to the law which changes.

The Formula of Concord expounds upon the third use of the law in a manner that is commensurate with Luther's explication of the law in his Large Catechism. God's law is not only a vertical reality, demonstrating the sinfulness of man before a holy God, but it also has an important horizontal dimension. The law of God is his unchanging will for his creation. It serves as a guide for Christians, informing them of God's perfect will. Though it does not, in itself, grant the power to obey, which is only through the Spirit received in the proclamation of the gospel, it does continue to function in the Christian life. By the law, believers constrain their sinful flesh, so that they are not obedient to their sinful desires. They are also guided in this life so that they live in the horizontal realm in a God-pleasing manner.

## Conclusion

The various confessional documents of Lutheranism have been here examined, and within these documents, it is apparent that the distinction between the two kinds of righteousness is a genuine extrapolation from historic Lutheran teaching. In his Large Catechism, Luther argues that one's life in the world is to be guided by the law. This law does not justify before God, but it serves as the guide by which Christians are to live in the world among other fellow creatures. The Ten Commandments are described, primarily, as a *coram mundo* reality, and their purpose is not only to condemn. The sacraments offer both forgiveness *coram Deo* and the ability to obey God's will *coram mundo*. By God's grace, the Christian begins to fulfill the law of God and does so to a greater degree throughout the life of faith. The Augsburg Confession demonstrates a similar concern for good works in expounding upon their necessity in the Christian life and their role as a guide in opposition to false good works taught by the Papists. In the Apology, Melanchthon utilizes explicit "two-kinds-of-righteousness" terminology in relation to philosophic, or civil, righteousness, and passive righteousness. Philosophic righteousness guides one in the world, but only passive righteousness has any merit before God. Melanchthon also distinguishes between the civil righteousness of pagans and the sanctification of the Christian believer. The Formula of Concord speaks explicitly about two kinds of righteousness in relation to alien righteousness, and the righteousness by which God indwells the Christian. This indwelling righteousness demonstrates itself through growth in sanctification and obedience to God's law when functioning in its third use.

In the Lutheran csonfessional documents, the two kinds of righteousness is a continual theme, just as the distinction between law and gospel is. This is not an occasional teaching, but it underlies several central sections of each confessional document. It is rightly viewed as a paradigm which frames a significant portion of Lutheran theology and practice. The contemporary emphasis on the two kinds of righteousness is thus validated, though some differences remain between the confessional teaching and that of some modern writers.

# The Two Kinds of Righteousness in Lutheran Orthodoxy

The two kinds of righteousness is a teaching which has recently been revived. However, this does not mean that the essence of this teaching is not present in historic Lutheran orthodoxy. There are several intimations of this teaching in the time between the writing of the Formula of Concord in the sixteenth century and the works of Wingren in the twentieth century. The teaching I have proposed is thoroughly consistent with traditional Lutheran theological categories. There are three specific places wherein this teaching is propounded in Lutheran orthodoxy. First, the scholastics distinguish between two different powers, or effects, of faith: justification and good works. Second, the Lutheran orthodox distinguish between justification (imputed righteousness), and sanctification (inherent righteousness). Third, some dogmaticians have distinguished between the *unio fidei formalis* and the *unio mystica* as two aspects of union with Christ that correspond to passive and active righteousness, respectively. The Lutheran dogmaticians are concerned not only with *coram Deo* justification, but with the Christian's life in this world according to God's moral will.

## The Twofold Effect of Faith

Faith has a twofold power. On the one hand, *coram Deo*, faith receives the righteousness of Christ. On the other, *coram mundo*, faith is operative in love. Heinrich Schmid describes the faith which saves as special faith, as opposed to general faith.[1] Special faith trusts in the promise of the gospel

---

1. Schmid defines this general faith as "a belief in general, that God is just and merciful, and has sent His Son into the world as Redeemer, but without any specific application of these truths" (Schmid, *Doctrinal Theology*, 411).

and saves. True and saving faith is not within man's power, but is a monergistic action on God's part.[2] Faith does not only justify before God, but it also produces good works. Heinrich Schmid contends that anywhere that God grants the gift of faith, a process of renewal and moral transformation begins.[3] All who have faith obtain both imputed and inherent righteousness. Good works are a necessary result of the work of God within man and flow forth from faith. These good works are in no way the ground of salvation, but its effect. Where good works are lacking, so is faith. Schmid notes that "where this [a changed life] is wanting we may assume that the faith is not of the right kind, and that the offered salvation has not really been appropriated."[4] Though one should not base one's assurance on good works, the neglect of good works demonstrates a lack of faith and salvation.

Schmid cites several scholastic theologians regarding the passive power of faith. David Hollaz writes:

> For justifying faith is the receptive organ and, as it were, the hand of the poor sinner, by which he applies and takes to himself, lays hold of, and possesses those things which are proffered in the free promise of the Gospel. God, the supreme Monarch, extends from heaven the hand of grace, obtained by the merit of Christ, and in it offers salvation. The sinner, in the abyss of misery, receives, as a beggar, in his hand of faith, what is thus offered to him. The offer and the reception are correlatives. Therefore the hand of faith, which seizes and appropriates the offered treasure, corresponds to the hand of grace which offers the treasure of righteousness and salvation.[5]

Faith saves, not because it has any inherent virtuous power within itself, but because it serves as an instrument of reception. *Coram Deo*, man cannot work for salvation, but receives, as a beggar, the gift of Christ's righteousness. Johannes Quenstedt further expounds upon the gracious nature of faith by noting that "faith proceeds from God, who regenerates, and is not the product of our own will; it is not meritorious. It has its origin in grace, not in nature; it is adventitious, not hereditary; supernatural, not

2. Ibid.

3. Ibid.

4. Ibid., 412.

5. As cited in Schmid, *Doctrinal Theology*, 420.

natural."[6] One's relationship to God, regarding both the origin of faith and the righteousness it receives, is passive.

David Hollaz is the first to distinguish explicitly between the two powers of faith, which Schmid notes is "very striking." He states, "The power and energy of faith are twofold, *receptive*, or apprehensive, and *operative*. The former is that by which faith passively receives Christ and everything obtained by His merit . . . The latter is that by which faith manifests itself actively by works of love and the practice of other virtues."[7] This distinction is nearly identical to the contemporary iterations of the two kinds of righteousness. Before God, faith merely receives. Before the world, faith performs; it is operative in love toward the neighbor. Johannes Brentz similarly argues that faith has "two hands." One hand extends upward toward God and receives his gifts. The other reaches down into the world of fellow man and performs works of love.[8] If one's faith is *not* operative, that indicates that such a faith is not real. Hollaz contends that "Faith ought to increase and be confirmed amid such terrors and other distresses. It can not therefore exist in those who live after the flesh, who delight in carnal lusts to obey them."[9] It is of the nature of faith that good deeds will be performed, not for justification, but for the good of the neighbor.

Revere Franklin Weidner also adopts Hollaz's distinction between the two powers of faith, distinguishing between the receptive aspect of faith, and faith as active and working.[10] In justification, faith is purely receptive. It does not work to merit justification. Rather, "it is the receptive organ, it is the hand of the soul, the hand moved by divinely given power by which it receives and applies grace to itself."[11] He likens faith to a hand which lays itself open to receive treasure from an outside source. It is in this passive righteousness of faith that one should place one's assurance, especially as such faith is granted through the means of grace. Yet, before the world, faith is also active in love. Weidner argues that all believers have operating faith. This is the necessary beginning of new spiritual life given through the creation of faith.[12] There are degrees of faith in regards to one's sanctification,

---

6. As cited in ibid.

7. As cited in ibid., 423.

8. Ibid.

9. As cited in ibid., 422.

10. Weidner, *Pneumatology*, 138.

11. Ibid., 138.

12. Ibid., 138–39.

but those degrees of faith are irrelevant to the perfect work of justification, which is dependent not on the strength of faith, but on its object.[13]

The distinction between the twofold power of faith is also adopted by Joseph Stump. He differentiates between faith's twofold effect and faith's twofold power. He writes that "The effect of faith is twofold, namely justification and sanctification."[14] Both justification and sanctification are received by faith. In justification, one receives the merit and righteousness of Christ; in sanctification, one is renewed in manner of life and inward affections.[15] There is, then, corresponding to the twofold effect of faith, a twofold power of faith. Stump contends that "saving faith is at once a receptive and operative power. As a receptive power it receives grace and forgiveness from God. As an operative power it worketh by love."[16] All true and saving faith has these two aspects. Stump, like Schmid, utilizes Brentz's analogy of the two hands of faith. With one, it accepts God's mercy in Christ (*coram Deo*), and with the other, works of love and service are performed in this world (*coram mundo*).[17] The receptive power of faith corresponds to justification, and its active power corresponds to sanctification. Faith implies a work of the Spirit in the sinner's heart, wherein one's being and disposition are changed. Stump contends that "the very existence of faith in the heart implies a new and right disposition toward God and an honest endeavor to do His will."[18] The lack of such a love of God means that faith is not present. He calls good works "the natural and inevitable result of true faith."[19] These good works do not in any way contribute to justification, but they demonstrate the reality of faith. Yet, even though works are signs of the presence of faith, Stump urges Christians not to look within for assurance. He writes, "When we ask, 'Am I saved?' we should not look within to see

13. Weidner cites Hollaz, who writes, "Faith is weak or infirm, when either a feeble light of the knowledge of Christ glimmers in the intellect, or the promise of grace is received with a languid and weak assent, or confidence struggles with an alarmed conscience. So Mark 9:24. But yet a weak faith may be true; as a spark concealed under the ashes is true fire, and a tender infant is a true human being. A strong and firm faith is a clear knowledge of the divine mercy, offered in Christ, a solid assent, and intrepid confidence overcoming all terrors" (ibid., 145).

14. Stump, *Christian Faith*, 214.

15. Ibid.

16. Ibid.

17. Ibid.

18. Ibid., 215.

19. Ibid.

whether we believe in Christ, but we should look to Christ and say, 'There is my righteousness and my salvation.' We are saved by confidently relying on Christ, and not by believing that we are relying on Him."[20] Passive rather than active righteousness is the grounds for Christian assurance. There are degrees of faith, and Christians should strive and pray for strengthening in their faith. Yet, these degrees of faith only relate to sanctification, or active righteousness. Regarding justification, a weak faith avails unto righteousness in the same manner as mature faith. The strength of faith is irrelevant to justification; rather the benefit of faith is Christ whom it grasps.[21] Before God, there are no degrees, but all are justified by the perfect righteousness of Christ.

This distinction between the twofold power of faith is essentially an expansion upon Luther's teaching on the two kinds of righteousness. Before God, faith is passive and receptive. Faith receives the free righteousness of Christ and the believer is thereby justified. On the other hand, faith performs good works. If there are no works, then faith is not genuine. These works do not contribute to one's standing *coram Deo*, but are active in the world for the good of others. Faith both justifies and sanctifies. It is in this particular distinction that a vertical/horizontal divide is more clearly made in Lutheran orthodox theologians. Though they do not use the language of "relationship," they explain life before God as one of passivity, and in the world as one of active works of service. The contemporary explanation of the two kinds of righteousness as a means by which one differentiates between the divine-human and human-human relationship is a valid explication and outgrowth of the theme of the twofold powers of faith in historic Lutheran discourse.

## The Doctrine of Sanctification

The doctrine of sanctification is an essential one in Lutheran orthodoxy. It is not negated or downplayed due to the centrality of justification in the Lutheran theological system. In discussions of the *ordo salutis*, Lutheran theologians have placed sanctification after justification as an essential element of God's redeeming work within the human creature. Salvation is both forensic and renovative. Justification is a legal term, referring to the imputation of Christ's righteousness and the forgiveness of sins; sanctification is

20. Ibid., 219.
21. Ibid., 216.

about inherent righteousness which actually changes the believer inwardly. The various discussions about sanctification demonstrate that the historic Lutheran tradition is concerned with both faith and life.

The terms "renovation" and "sanctification" are both used to describe the process whereby a Christian grows in grace. These terms are often used interchangeably,[22] but some have argued that they refer to two different aspects of the same movement. Weidner asserts that renovation refers to the negative aspect of man's change, and sanctification to the positive.[23] Schmid writes, "This operation, however, wrought by God in man, is called renovation, so far as through it a change is wrought by God in man; also sanctification, so far as now his life begins to become holy."[24] Renovation consists in the putting off of sin, and sanctification to the inherent holiness that is wrought in man. Conrad Lindberg further explains these distinctions:

> *Renovatio negativa* or *sanctificatio stride dicta* is that part of the grace of renovation by which the power of sin is ever increasingly overcome and the old Adam is put off or dies, although slowly. *Renovatio positiva* or *sanctificatio strictissime dicta* is therefore the gracious act of the Spirit through which He renews in man the image of God, while man co-operates with the powers granted in regeneration. Renovation is therefore considered both from the transitive and intransitive point of view.[25]

Both of these aspects of Christian growth continue throughout the believer's life.

There have generally been two separate meanings applied to the term "sanctification." In one sense, sanctification can be used broadly, in reference to the entire process whereby the Holy Spirit applies the redemption accomplished by Christ in the *ordo salutis*, as Luther uses the term in his Small Catechism.[26] This sense of the term is not utilized extensively by the

22. "Note that the Formula of Concord uses the terms 'renewal' and 'sanctification' as synonyms" (Pieper, *Christian Dogmatics*, III.4–5).

23. Weidner, *Pneumatology*, 181.

24. Schmid, *Doctrinal Theology*, 486.

25. Lindberg, *Christian Dogmatics*, 356.

26. Stump, *Christian Faith*, 276. Pieper gives a more extensive definition of the broad sense of sanctification: "In its wide sense, sanctification comprises all that the Holy Ghost does in separating man from sin and making him again God's own, so that he may live for God and serve Him. It includes the bestowal of faith, justification, sanctification as the inner transformation of man, perseverance in faith, and the complete Renewal on

Lutheran scholastics, though some theologians do admit that this is the more common biblical usage of the term "sanctification."[27] Apart from this broad sense, sanctification is used to refer to the progress of the believer in a life of holiness. This is its usual meaning in classic Lutheranism. Stump defines sanctification with the following words: "Sanctification is that work of the Holy Spirit by which the believer, cooperating with God through powers divinely bestowed in regeneration, grows in personal holiness by more and more overcoming sin in his heart and life and by cultivating the Christian graces and virtues."[28] Pieper defines sanctification this way: "In its narrow sense, sanctification designates the internal spiritual transformation of the believer or the holiness of life which follows upon justification."[29] Similarly, Adolf Hoenecke defines sanctification as "that activity of appropriating the grace of the Holy Spirit by virtue of which the justified person day to day lays aside the sinful nature still clinging to him, and day by day is renewed according to God's image and lives for God in holiness and righteousness."[30] There is broad agreement in the Lutheran tradition surrounding the narrow sense of sanctification.[31]

In its narrow sense, sanctification is a progressive action. Gerberding writes that "sanctification being a work in which man has a share, is progressive."[32] Pieper notes that "Scripture admonishes us to grow, increase, abound, in sanctification."[33] Unlike justification, sanctification is not a perfect act of God. It is a renovative one, and grows throughout the Christian life.[34] One will not, however, achieve perfection in this life. The Lutheran dogmaticians have been unanimous in rejecting any type of Christian perfectionism. Quenstedt contends that "renovation in this life is

---

Judgment Day" (Pieper, *Christian Dogmatics* III:3).

27. "In the New Testament use of the term sanctification does not mean a progress in holiness, much less a progress into holiness" (Voigt, *Biblical Dogmatics*, 183).

28. Stump, *Christian Faith*, 276.

29. Pieper, *Christian Dogmatics* III:4.

30. Hoenecke, *Evangelical Lutheran Dogmatics* III:395.

31. A more classic definition comes from Abraham Calov, which is essentially the same as those cited above: "the work of the Holy Trinity, by which He consecrates us in soul and body filling us with virtues of every kind, and expelling vices of every kind, and brings to us the grace of God and kingdom of heaven." (cited in Jacobs, *Summary*, 248).

32. Gerberding, *Way of Salvation*, 188.

33. Pieper, *Christian Dogmatics* III:31.

34. "Inasmuch as renovation is progressive and therefore continually developing, it must have degrees" (Lindberg, *Christian Dogmatics*, 357).

partial and imperfect, admitting degrees, and therefore it never attains the highest acme of perfection."[35] The fact that such perfect renovation will not occur in this life is not an excuse to cease attempting to grow. Pieper writes, "On the contrary, it is God's will and the will of the Christian that he strive after perfection; he wants to be fruitful, not only in some, but in all good works."[36] Growth in the Christian faith is not a neglected topic in Lutheranism, but is consistently taught by Lutheran theologians.

Christians work with God in the process of sanctification. Hoenecke writes that the process is synergistic, but the only reason why the human creature has any ability to cooperate with God is God's prior works of grace.[37] In the Lutheran tradition, sanctification is *not* described as monergistic. The believer *does* play a role in Christian growth and obedience. Yet, this role is a secondary one. Hollaz, for example, argues that the Holy Trinity is the primary efficient cause in sanctification. It is God who grants the ability to perform good works, and it is God who initiates, continues, and finishes the process. Yet, man does cooperate as a secondary cause, as he is moved by the Holy Spirit. Hollaz states, "The regenerate man cooperates with God in the work of sanctification, not by an equal action, but in subordination and dependence on the Holy Spirit, because he works, not *with native*, but with *granted powers*."[38] It is in this sense that theologians argue that believers can renew themselves. A distinction has sometimes been made between transitive and intransitive renovation. Transitive renovation refers to the fact that God has granted new spiritual abilities to the human creature, without which any Christian growth is impossible. Intransitive renovation is the reality that believers renew themselves in the image of God. Intransitive renovation is based on transitive, because apart from God's prior and continuing action, such renovation would not be possible.[39]

There are various ways of explaining the continuing reality of sanctification in the life of the Christian. The language of the new and old man is common among Lutheran theologians. Jacobs defines the "old man" as "the remnants of the corrupt nature in all parts and powers of the regenerate man, darkness and perversity of intellect, disordered affections, emotions,

---

35. Schmid, *Doctrinal Theology*, 490.
36. Pieper, *Christian Dogmatics* III:30.
37. Hoenecke, *Lutheran Dogmatics* III:400.
38. Cited in Schmid, *Doctrinal Theology*, 491.
39. Ibid., 487.

appetites, the self-centered disposition of man."[40] As one grows in sanctification, the old man is put off. The new man is "the restored image of God" that continues to increase.[41] Throughout the Christian's life, the old man dies, and the new is raised to life. Though the old sinful nature continues to exist until death, its power does weaken. Quenstedt argues, "The old man is the starting-point (*terminus a quo*), the new man the goal (*terminus ad quem*)."[42] The existence of the old and new man does not suggest that there are two separate persons in a Nestorian fashion, but these are figurative references to the sinful and righteous aspects of the renewed Christian. Hollaz explains:

> As the body of sin in process of time is more and more weakened by the regenerate man, so the regenerate man is transformed more and more into the image of God from glory to glory by the Holy Spirit (2 Cor. 3:18; 4:46). The body of sin, Rom. 6:6, is called figuratively the old man, as it is a compound of many sins, as of parts and members. As formerly criminals were affixed to the cross, and their limbs bruised, mortified, buried, and corrupted, so successfully the old man is crucified when the desires of his flesh are restrained and as if bound; he is bruised, 1 Cor. 9:27, so far as the flesh is kept under, the external pleasures of this world being removed; being bruised, he is mortified, Rom. 8:13, so far as the strength to emerge is taken from sin; mortified he is buried, Rom. 6:4, inasmuch as the memory and the thought of illicit things are removed; buried, he corrupts, so that the entire body of sin is abolished, here inchoately and continuously, in the life to come completely.[43]

This process includes the mortification of sin, and the vivification of the new man, and is also referred to as the renewal of the *imago Dei* which was lost at the fall. C. F. W. Walther argues that this renewal in the image of God is the very purpose of redemption. Walther contends, "God's Son appeared in this world for no other reason but to restore God's work which was destroyed, to bring back what we have lost, in a word, to restore us in the divine image of which we were robbed."[44] The death of the old man and

40. Jacobs, *Summary*, 249.
41. Ibid.
42. Cited in Schmid, *Doctrinal Theology*, 505.
43. Cited in Schmid, *Doctrinal Theology*, 490.
44. Walther, *Selected Sermons*, 19.

the renewal of the *imago Dei* are not tertiary soteriological themes, but are central to human redemption.

Several important distinctions should be noted among the scholastic theologians regarding sanctification. A distinction is made between the vital and active principles of sanctification.[45] The vital principle, or that which gives life to sanctification as its cause, is faith. Faith brings new life, and only through this new spiritual vitality can good works be performed. The active principle refers to the manner in which sanctification is demonstrated: love. These two principles always coexist in the renewed Christian. The scholastics argue that there are several means of sanctification. The primary means of renovation is the word of God. Quenstedt explicates four manners in which the word sanctifies.[46] First, the Holy Spirit, who causes sanctification, works through his word. Second, the word is both effective and extensive in sanctification, both granting the beginning of the work and bringing it to completion. Third, the word guides sanctification as a norm. The word "not only divinely shows the good commandments and actions pleasing to God, but also directs the renewed will of man into zeal for good works."[47] Finally, the word works in sanctification animatedly, because Christians are animated by the kindness of God shown in the gospel which causes them to perform good works. The word of God sanctifies as both law and gospel, and each of these aspects of Scripture functions in a different manner. The law prescribes the good works which are to be performed, and the gospel grants the Holy Spirit, through whom good works are possible.[48] Along with God's word, the sacraments also serve as instruments of sanctification, through which holiness is increased.

## Differences between Justification and Sanctification

The two kinds of righteousness is essentially another manner in which to discuss the difference between justification and sanctification. Both of these

---

45. Stump, *Christian Faith*, 281–82.

46. This is cited in Hoenecke, *Evangelical Lutheran Dogmatics* III:399.

47. Hoenecke, *Evangelical Lutheran Dogmatics* III:399.

48. "Thus according to these Scripture passages the Holy Spirit works sanctification through all of God's Word (2 Ti 3:16, 17), on the one hand through the law as teaching of what sanctification is and on the other hand through the gospel, which effects the power of sanctification and love through which alone the Holy Spirit works everything (Gal 5:21) and constantly comes to us (Gal 3:2)" (ibid., 398–99).

realities involve righteousness, and both are necessary parts of salvation. Yet, they are distinct. Justification involves the imputation of righteousness, whereas sanctification includes actual righteousness which grows in the believer, causing him to perform good works. In nearly every scholastic treatment of the doctrine of sanctification, there is a section outlining several of the major differences between these two acts.

Francis Pieper enumerates a number of important differences between justification and sanctification. Justification is an act that occurs outside of the human subject. It is a divine judgment, whereby one is declared righteous. It is not about an inner change within the creature, but a forensic verdict. It is in justification that faith and works are in opposition to one another, as one is justified solely by faith. In contrast to this, sanctification is a work of God which happens within the human creature "(*in homine*)."[49] This inner change produces good works. Pieper distinguishes then between *iustitia imputata* (imputed righteousness), and *iustitia inhaerens* (inherent righteousness). Both of these realities are true righteousness, but they serve different functions for the Christian. Imputed righteousness defines one's standing before God, and inherent righteousness defines one's life in good works.

Johannes Quenstedt offers six points to differentiate justification from sanctification. First, these acts are distinct regarding their efficient cause. Justification is caused solely by God, but sanctification is a cooperative effort between God and man. They also differ as to the subject. Justification concerns man insofar as he is apart from grace, whereas sanctification regards the already justified Christian. Third, the objects of both acts differ. Justification is about imputed righteousness, whereas sanctification regards inherent righteousness. Fourth, the form differs. Justification is the imputation of Christ's righteousness and the forgiveness of sins, and sanctification is "the reformation of the mind, will, and affections, and so of the whole man, or in the restoration of the divine image, commenced in this life and to be completed in the next."[50] Fifth, the properties differ. Justification is instantaneous, and sanctification is progressive. Finally, the order differs. Justification is the cause of sanctification, but sanctification is not the cause of justification.

Though justification and sanctification are distinct, they are not separate. Pieper contends that "There is an inseparable connection (*nexus*

49. Pieper, *Christian Dogmatics* III:6.
50. Weidner, *Pneumatology*, 182.

*indivulsus*) between justification and sanctification."[51] The justified Christian is also the sanctified Christian. No one can be justified without at the same time have the beginnings of renewal worked within him. Both sanctification and justification are worked in the believer at the same moment, yet there is a causal relationship between justification and sanctification.[52] This connection is partially a psychological one, as Pieper notes that the willingness to obey God's will is increased through contemplation of divine mercy. The gospel increases one's affections toward God and motivation to perform good deeds.[53] Justification and sanctification are also connected in that the Spirit uses faith as the instrument to perform both acts.

Adolf Hoenecke mentions three ways in which justification is related to the Christian's growth in sanctification. First, like Pieper, Hoenecke notes that there is a psychological connection. The justification of the sinner causes one to rejoice in God's will and seek to obey him out of thanksgiving. Second, Hoenecke argues that justification does not refer only to the imputation of righteousness, but also to the reality of adoption. The Spirit of adoption is the one who grants a life of good works (Gal 4:6). Thus, justification and sanctification are connected in that it is the Spirit who applies both realities to the Christian. Third, the objective acts of Christ which justify are applied subjectively to the believer, not only by imputation, but also by participation. Hoenecke argues that "through fellowship with Christ, that which happened to Christ for our justification is also to happen to us who are justified, namely, death and resurrection."[54] The connection between justification and sanctification is Christ himself. Hoenecke explains: "It is also the doctrine of Scripture that, as we in faith bear the form of the perfectly righteous Christ before God by virtue of imputation of justification, so also the same righteous Christ is to be formed in those who are justified."[55] Through faith, Christ both justifies and sanctifies.

Another manner in which dogmaticians have distinguished between the acts of justification and sanctification is by propounding the difference between operating and cooperating grace. David Hollaz expounds upon

---

51. Pieper, *Christian Dogmatics* III:7.

52. "The Apostle certainly teaches that there is an indissoluble connection between sanctification, or the *iustitia inhaerens*, and justification, the mere imputation of righteousness" (ibid. III:9).

53. Ibid. III:10.

54. Hoenecke, *Evangelical Lutheran Dogmatics* III:382.

55. Ibid.

six different aspects of grace that are applied to the sinner: prevenient, preparing, operating, cooperating, preserving, and glorifying grace. Operating grace relates to regeneration, justification, and union with God. These are monergistic acts of God, wherein he grants faith and salvation to the unbelieving sinner. This is distinct from cooperating grace, which Hollaz defines as "that act of grace wherein the Holy Spirit acts concurrently with the justified man to sanctification, and the bringing forth of good works."[56] This is sanctification. Quenstedt makes a similar distinction, using the terms "operating grace" and "indwelling grace."[57] These two kinds of grace are virtually synonymous with the two kinds of righteousness in Luther's thought. Operating grace is the work of God, wherein the sinner is passive. Cooperative, or indwelling, grace is a work in which man is active in striving for obedience.

## Good Works

The notion of good works is intimately connected with the doctrine of sanctification. These two topics are often discussed in the same loci. In the older works, such as those of Melanchthon, Chemnitz, and Gerhard, good works are treated after justification as the two primary distinct topics in salvation. Later writers who employ the *ordo salutis* as an ordering structure for soteriological discussion place good works within the topic of sanctification.

The debate surrounding the nature of good works was at the heart of the Reformation, and therefore was an important defining point within the developing Lutheran tradition. David Hollaz gives the following definition:

> Good works are free acts of justified persons, performed through the renewing grace of the Holy Spirit, according to the prescription of the divine law, through faith in Christ preceding, to the honor of God and the edification of men . . . By works here are understood not only external visible actions, such as precede from the hand or tongue, but internal affections of the heart and movements of the will, and thus the entire obedience and inherent righteousness of the regenerate. Internal good works are seen by the eyes of God alone, and comprise the inner thoughts of the mind, the movements of the will, and the pure affection of the heart, such

56. As cited in Weidner, *Pneumatology*, 25.
57. As cited in ibid., 26.

as love, the fear of God, confidence toward God, patience, humility. The external good works are seen not only by God, but likewise
by man, and manifest themselves by outward demeanor, words,
and actions . . . A good intention is to be accounted among good
internal works.[58]

Good works consist both in the intention and attitude of the person performing them, and the external act performed.

The Lutheran scholastic tradition affirms, along with Luther, the
sole sufficiency of faith in one's relationship to God. Justification comes
to the sinner *sola fide*. As Junius Remensnyder writes, "Scripture teaches
definitely and cumulatively that the ground of our justification is solely and
absolutely the blood and righteousness of Christ, and that the condition
or means of our justification is faith which lays hold upon the great 'pro-
pitiation for sinners.'"[59] These good works do not contribute to salvation,
and they are not the cause of maintaining salvation gained by faith. Yet,
even though works are completely excluded as grounds for justification,
the Lutheran dogmaticians consistently emphasize their necessity in the
Christian life. Francis Pieper mentions that some have rejected the phrase
"sanctification and good works are necessary," but contends that this statement is consistent with the teachings of Scripture.[60] The biblical writers
consistently testify to the necessity of good works in the Christian life.
Pieper defines this necessity by expounding upon three reasons why God
commands holy living. First, God commands it on his own account. God
desires service toward him rather than toward Satan or any other master.
Second, Christians should perform good works on their own account.
By good works, believers testify to the genuineness of their faith. Finally,
Christians should perform good works for the sake of others, so that the
truth of the gospel might be seen through holy actions.[61] Hoenecke further
expounds upon the nature of necessity regarding good works.[62] He argues
that good deeds are necessary in four ways. First, they are necessitated by
God's command. They are not given in the divine law arbitrarily, or as mere
adiaphora. Rather, they must be obeyed. Second, they are necessitated in
that man is obligated to obey what God commands by way of debt. Third,

58. As cited in Weidner, *Pneumatology*, 185.

59. Remensnyder, *Lutheran Manual*, 33.

60. Pieper, *Christian Dogmatics* III:28.

61. Ibid., III.29.

62. Hoenecke, *Evangelical Lutheran Dogmatics* III:417.

good works are necessary by the order of salvation. Regeneration always results in a new life of obedience. Without this new obedience, salvation has not been received. Fourth, they have a necessity of presence in relation to faith. If faith is present, good works must also be present as the manner in which faith demonstrates itself.

Conrad Lindberg mentions several important distinctions that the scholastic theologians make in reference to good works.[63] He notes that good works can be divided into two classes: *interna* (internal) and *externa* (external). In their most absolute sense, good works are judged according to the law of God, which is the standard of moral actions. Because of the pervasiveness of sin, however, the form of good works consists not only in their conformity with God's law, but also in the believer's faith in Christ who covers imperfection with his perfect righteousness. Both the external act and the internal faith of the Christian are parts of the essence of a believer's good deeds. Lindberg further divides good works into three different categories, relating to their relative goodness. First, there is the internal motivation of the heart in performing good deeds. This, only God himself is able to see. Second are those works that conform to the first table of the law and consist in love toward God. Finally, some good works are specifically for the love of neighbor and thus conform to the second table of God's law.

It is also the consistent testimony of Lutheran theologians that God grants rewards for the Christian's good deeds. The service that one provides for the neighbor, as well as the persecution that Christians face, will be rewarded in heaven. Yet, the reward of good works is not a reward of necessity. Even the best works of the Christian are tainted by sin, and thus "this reward, so Scripture further instructs us, must be regarded strictly as a reward of grace."[64] Pieper expounds upon this as a twofold truth: first, God rewards good works, and second, one can never claim these rewards as a right based on the good deeds performed.[65] Joseph Stump summarizes Scripture's teaching on this subject: "But it will be a reward of grace and not of merit; a reward, *not for* the deeds, but *according* to the deeds."[66]

Good works are not a tertiary discussion within Lutheranism, but are a central aspect of Christian life and preaching. Francis Pieper notes that

63. Lindberg, *Christian Dogmatics*, 359–62.

64. Pieper, *Christian Dogmatics* III:52.

65. Ibid. III:52.

66. Stump, *Christian Faith*, 288.

the sinful flesh always desires to avoid performing good works, and to prevent this, one should look for every opportunity to perform good deeds.[67] Though good works are spontaneous in that they flow from a willing spirit, a Christian is called to exercise his will in performing them. There is discontinuity here between Pieper and Wingren, who de-emphasizes effort in works of love toward the neighbor. Pieper states, "Scripture speaks not only to the quality of good works but also has much to say of their quantity."[68] The Christian should continue to strive to perform more and more good deeds. It is the duty of the Christian pastor to encourage his people to do so. Pieper argues that "in urging the members of their churches to become 'rich in good works,' pastors should not be deterred from doing this boldly and resolutely, without any fear or faltering, by the thought that this insistence on good works might crowd out of its central position the doctrine of justification without works."[69] So long as justification *coram Deo* is continually emphasized and remains central, there should be no fear of exhorting parishioners unto good works. C. F. W. Walther offers these bold words regarding those who believe that they can hold onto the doctrine of justification *sola fide* while neglecting the importance of good deeds:

> Consequently we dare not think that God's Son became a man only to fulfill the Law for us by His holy life. He did not suffer for our sins and die on the cross only to win for us the forgiveness of our sins, to deliver us from the punishment we deserve, to reconcile us with God, and despite our sins unlock heaven and salvation to us. This is how many see Christ. They, therefore, seek nothing in Christ but comfort for their restless conscience. That they should actually again become holy is of no concern to them at all. However, they are caught in a great most dangerous error.[70]

Good works are essential to the Christian life, not to earn or retain salvation, but so that the Christian might live *coram mundo* in a God-pleasing manner.

67. Pieper, *Christian Dogmatics*, III, 47.
68. Ibid. III:47.
69. Ibid. III:48.
70. Walther, *Selected Sermons*, 21.

## The Mystical Union

The doctrine of the *unio mystica* is essential for understanding the two distinct forms of righteousness taught within the Lutheran tradition. Passive righteousness is an *extra nos* reality, relating to the imputation of Christ's alien righteousness in justification. Active righteousness is an *intra nos* reality, relating to the indwelling of the Holy Trinity within the Christian. An understanding of the *unio mystica* helps to elucidate the difference between the good works of the Christian and those of the unbeliever. For the Christian, good works are performed by the indwelling Trinity, wherein God causes the believer to be formed into Christ's image.

The earliest Lutheran writers did not explicitly distinguish between various benefits of the *ordo salutis*, and thus they did not include separate aspects of the application of redemption in various loci. This does not mean, however, that the mystical union was absent from early sources. Johann Gerhard, for example, explains this teaching extensively in his various devotional writings. For Gerhard, salvation is not limited to forensic metaphors. He explicates an approach to redemption which is centered not only on the cross as a vicarious satisfaction, but also on the incarnation as the union between God and man. He notes, "The Savior himself was clothed in the flesh so that, by communicating the glory of divinity to the flesh, he could purify the sinful flesh, so that, by the healing power of his perfect righteousness that was communicated to the flesh, he could purge the poisonous quality of sin inherent in our flesh, and in this way obtain grace for our flesh."[71] Through Christ's incarnation, he deified humanity. This theosis language is consistent in Gerhard's writings, wherein he argues that love makes the lover more like the beloved. He writes, "Love unites and love changes . . . If you love God and the divine, you will become divine. Love of God is the chariot of Elijah ascending into heaven."[72] This indwelling righteousness of Christ which transforms the Christian is just as much a reality as divine imputation. Christ both won salvation on the cross and also "entered into me and worked through my whole substance."[73] The theme of union with Christ is consistent in Gerhard's writings. Faith

71. Gerhard, *Sacred Meditations*, 25.
72. Ibid., 48.
73. Ibid., 43.

"implants us into our Savior"[74] and "weds us to Christ."[75] This union with Christ is the source for the Christian's life of obedience.[76]

The doctrine of the mystical union was formalized in the high scholastic era by Quenstedt, Calov, and Hollaz, who placed the *unio mystica* within their discussions of the *ordo salutis* following justification in connection with *renovatio*. David Hollaz defines the mystical union as "the spiritual conjunction of the triune God with justified man, by which He dwells in him as in a consecrated temple by His special presence, and that, too, substantial, and operates in the same by his gracious influence."[77] The two primary elements of the mystical union are the indwelling of God and the internal change that the Christian experiences through this influence. In terms of union's place within the *ordo salutis*, there are two separate proposals among the Lutheran scholastics. Schmid cites Quenstedt as asserting that mystical union follows justification, yet precedes sanctification and renovation as their cause. Hollaz affirms that in a sense, union with God arises as a result of justification. Yet, there is a sense in which a kind of union *precedes* justification. This is what Hollaz refers to as the *unio fidei formalis:* the formal union of faith. He notes that "the formal union of faith, by which Christ is apprehended, put on, and united with us, as the mediator and the author of grace and pardon, logically precedes justification."[78] This union of faith is not the *unio mystica*, but the uniting of the believer with Christ in faith, through which his benefits are given to the recipient. By distinguishing between these two manners of speaking about union, Hollaz speaks of union in two manners that cohere with the two kinds of righteousness. The *unio fidei formalis* is a passive-righteousness reality, wherein the believer is connected with Christ's righteousness for justification. The *unio mystica*, then, is an active-righteousness reality, wherein the Christian is internally changed by God's indwelling. A more simple way of distinguishing these two kinds of union is by describing the *unio fidei formalis* as "me in Christ," and the *unio mystica* as "Christ in me." By utilizing this distinction, Hollaz is able to affirm Luther's teaching of the

---

74. Ibid., 56.

75. Ibid., 58.

76. "When faith weds us to Christ, it unites us with Christ, and for that reason faith is the mother of all strength in us. Where faith is, there is Christ. Where Christ is, there is a holy life, namely, true humility, true gentleness and true love" (ibid., 58).

77. As cited in Schmid, *Doctrinal Theology*, 482.

78. As cited in ibid., 481.

marriage union that the believer participates in through faith, while also affirming the Formula of Concord's contention that renovative union is a result, rather than cause, of justification.

There are several important distinctions made by the Lutheran scholastics surrounding the teaching of the mystical union. First, there is a distinction between the *unitio* and the *unio*. The *unitio* is the initiating of one's union with God. This occurs at the same moment as regeneration and justification, yet logically follows justification, as justification follows regeneration. The *unio*, then, is one's growth in union that corresponds to sanctification and renovation.[79] There is also a distinction between a general union that God has with all men, and a special union, whereby God dwells specifically within believers. In the general union, God is present throughout his creation and works within all people, both believers and unbelievers. The special union is differentiated as divine indwelling, whereby God, by his grace, is present within believers. This distinction helps to explain the difference between the civil righteousness of the unbeliever and the inherent righteousness of the believer. They are both worked by God in some sense, but each in a different manner. Quenstedt mentions the special presence of the Holy Spirit in the form of the dove descending upon Christ versus the Spirit's general presence in the world as an example of this distinction. Schmid explains this distinction: "the union in general is not a mere gracious operation of the Holy Spirit, so the special union does not differ from the general merely by a new and special mode of operating, but by a new approximation of essence, and that distinct from the common mode of presence."[80] This special union is further divided into two separate categories: the gracious union and the glorious union. One's life in the church prior to eschatological glory consists of a gracious union. God unites himself to the believer, but not to such an extent that the Christian is perfectly conformed to God's image. The glorious union occurs upon death, wherein one's union with God is made perfect, and sin is eliminated. The dogmaticians are clear to differentiate the mystical union from pagan notions of union. This union does not involve the transformation of the substance of man into the substance of God. Quenstedt argues that the union of these two substances is not transubstantiation, wherein one substance becomes another, or consubstantiation, wherein a third substance is

79. Ibid., 482.
80. Ibid., 485.

created by two separate essences.[81] This union is also distinguished from the union of the two natures within the one person of Christ. Yet, this union is real and vital. It is not the mere union of wills, but the union of two substances, wherein there is "a true and real and most intimate conjunction of the divine and human nature of the theanthropic Christ with a regenerated man, which is effected by virtue of the merit of Christ through the Word and Sacraments."[82] Quenstedt further explains that it is "a true, real, intrinsic, and most close conjunction of the substance of the believer with the substance of the Holy Trinity and the flesh of Christ."[83] A common manner in which this is expressed is with a marriage metaphor. Calov argues, "The espousal of Christ with believers is that by which He eternally marries Himself to believers through faith, so that they become one spirit, and by His power communicates to them, as to His spiritual bride, intimate and enduring love, all His blessing and all His glory."[84] The Christian's union with God is true and real, yet it does not confuse the distinction between the creature and his Creator.

After the decline of seventeenth-century scholasticism, the doctrine of the mystical union was expounded upon by several nineteenth-and early-twentieth-century theologians. It is explained as a separate benefit of the Spirit in the writings of Schmid, Jacobs, Weidner, Stump, Lindberg, Valentine, Walther, and Hoenecke. Pieper mentions the mystical union but spends only a page and a half of his multivolume *Christian Dogmatics* on the teaching. Pieper refers to this union as an effect of justification, whereby the Holy Trinity indwells the Christian. This is distinct from the general union that God has with all creatures, but it is not a pantheistic union, whereby the substances of God and man are confused. Pieper also, in a footnote, mentions Hollaz's distinction between the *unio mystica* and the *unio fidei formalis*. He affirms this distinction by arguing that the union of faith is an external union, but the mystical union an internal one.[85] Though he does note that "the doctrine of the mystic union is highly important both as a doctrine and for the Christian life," he fails to expound upon this benefit, instead focusing on the forensic gift of justification.[86]

81. Ibid.
82. Calov, as cited in ibid., 482–83.
83. Cited in ibid., 483.
84. Cited in ibid.
85. Pieper, *Christian Dogmatics* II:434.
86. Pieper, *Christian Dogmatics* II:409.

Adolf Hoenecke, who like Pieper wrote a multivolume series on Christian dogmatics, devotes an extensive amount of space to the teaching of the mystical union. Avoiding reductionistic theological positions, Hoenecke affirms that the *unio mystica* is an essential aspect of the Christian's redemption as applied by the Holy Spirit. He defines the union in this way: "that the triune God through the Holy Spirit essentially is graciously present in believers, through which those thus united with God not only blessedly rejoice and are filled with comfort and peace but also are made constantly more certain in grace, strengthened in sanctification, and preserved for eternal life."[87] Throughout his work, Hoenecke utilizes the traditional distinctions as expounded upon by Calov and Hollaz.

What is particularly helpful in Hoenecke's work on the mystical union is his response to nineteenth-century rejections of the traditional Lutheran teaching. He mentions, for example, Alex Ottingen, who rejects the mystical union as metaphysical speculation unbefitting of Lutheran theology. Perhaps more important is Albrecht Ritschl's rejection of the mystical union as incompatible with his Kantian approach to Luther. For Ritschl, the union that the believer has with Christ is a mere union of wills, not a union of substances.[88] Hoenecke responds in two ways. First, he demonstrates that union language is not speculative, but is utilized throughout Scripture.[89] The language of the union of substances is not intended as an extensive explanation of the mechanics of such a union, but explicates the closeness and intimacy of the union between God and man. Second, Hoenecke shows that the teaching of mystical union is essential to Luther's theology. He demonstrates that Ritschl only cites the texts of Luther which are written against the speculative ideas about union expounded upon in such writers as Dionysius the Areopogite. In contradistinction to this, Hoenecke posits that Luther expounds upon a true teaching of union in his 1535 Galatians commentary.[90] Luther did not reject all forms of mysticism, but simply a speculative mysticism divorced from word and sacrament.

87. Hoenecke, *Evangelical Lutheran Dogmatics* III:385.

88. This criticism has been extensively discussed in the works of Tuomo Mannermaa and the other proponents of the Finnish interpretation of Luther. Hoenecke gives nearly the same responses as contemporary Finnish scholars, but precedes them by seventy years. It is unfortunate that Hoenecke has not been utilized more in this important discussion.

89. Hoenecke, *Evangelical Lutheran Dogmatics*, III: 385–86.

90. He cites the following section: "Faith takes hold of Christ and has him present, enclosing him as the ring encloses the gem. 'Not I, but Christ lives in me.' Christ

Joseph Stump is the latest dogmatician to expound upon the mystical union extensively within his dogmatics texts. In his 1932 book *The Christian Faith*, Joseph Stump professes a doctrine of mystical union that is consistent with earlier dogmatic theologians. Stump argues that this teaching is not new, but is contained implicitly in the Formula of Concord, although there is no specific article on or expansion of the topic within that document. Stump notes that the teaching was initially propounded for two reasons. First, the teaching of the *unio mystica* helps to guard against the false teaching of Caspar Schwenkfeld and others who were viewed as pantheistic, confusing the essences of God and man. Second, the mystical union affirms that which is true about the teachings of Osiander, Schwenkfeld, and Valentin Weigel. In this way, Stump argues that the mystical union guards against both an excessive mysticism and a notion of salvation that neglects participationist themes.[91]

Stump places the teaching of the mystical union within the *ordo salutis*, after regeneration, justification, and repentance. The believer is not only justified, but "Christ dwells in him, and through Christ the Holy Trinity."[92] This union occurs in two stages. First it is established at the same moment that one has faith and receives justification. Second, this union grows, as "the fullness of the experience is proportioned to the degree of faith and sanctification."[93] This division of the union in two stages mirrors the earlier distinction between the *unio* and *unitio*. The union which the believer has with Christ is the source and foundation for all sanctification and good works. Stump argues that the "branch grows and puts forth leaves and fruit; but it does so only because and as long as it is vitally united with the tree from which its life comes."[94] This union, which occurs by faith, is the source of all good works and Christian obedience. Like previous treatments of the doctrine, Stump affirms that this union is to be regarded, not merely

---

is my 'form,' which adorns my faith as color or light adorns a wall. (This fact has to be expounded in this crude way, for there is no spiritual way for us to grasp the idea that Christ clings and dwells in us as closely and intimately as light or whiteness clings to a wall.) . . . [T]his attachment to him causes me to be liberated from the terror of the law and of sin. But faith must be taught correctly, namely, that by it you are so cemented to Christ that he and you are as one person, which cannot be separated but remains attached to him forever" (Ibid., III:389).

91. This is all mentioned in Stump, *Christian Faith*, 272.

92. Ibid.

93. Ibid., 273.

94. Ibid., 274.

as a union of wills, but a union of two substances in vital relationship to one another. Yet this union avoids the mixing of two natures, so as to make man essentially divine.[95]

There is broad consensus among Lutheran theologians regarding the reality of the *unio mystica* and its importance in the Christian life. This is the means by which one grows in active righteousness and good works, as God works within and changes the believer. This internal change is then differentiated from the *unio fidei formalis*, whereby the Christian is united to Christ by faith, thus receiving his benefits. The distinction between the mystical union and the formal union of faith is another means in which the two kinds of righteousness are distinguished. The *unio mystica* relates to active righteousness, and the *unio fidei formalis* to passive righteousness.

## Civil Righteousness

Though it is not a particularly prominent topic, Lutheran theologians have argued that unbelievers can be righteous in an external sense. Unregenerate people have the ability to perform many works that benefit society, which God uses in his providence to sustain the world. Yet, these works are not truly good works in God's sight, because unbelievers' motives are not pure, and their imperfections are not covered by the blood of Christ in faith.

Francis Pieper has a particularly helpful section on the relationship between good works and the unregenerate in his *Christian Dogmatics*. Pieper confesses that unbelievers can perform good deeds that "comply externally (*in materia*) with the norm of the divine Law still written in the heart of fallen man."[96] He cites Romans 2:14 to demonstrate that there is a natural law, written on the heart, which all people can (to some extent) obey. Pieper argues that the distinction between the good works of the regenerate and unregenerate relate to Luther's two-kingdom theology. He states, "The best distinction between the good works of the heathen and those of Christians is made when the Lutheran Confessions assign these works to the wholly different spheres to which they actually belong. The good works of the heathen belong in the sphere of civil righteousness (*iustitia civilis*) or of the

---

95. "It is a real indwelling of God in man, a real union between them, which the old dogmaticians described as a union of substance with substance, but which they took care to guard against the notion that the divine and human substances are confused or amalgamated" (ibid., 275).

96. Pieper, *Christian Dogmatics* III:43.

State."[97] The unbeliever does many good works in the civil realm, which benefit society. However, these good works, though good in some sense *co-ram mundo*, have no benefit spiritually. While the Christian performs good works that are *tainted* by sin, for the unbeliever, all works are *properly* sins. There is an immense difference between the righteousness of a Christian and pagan.

The unbeliever's works are considered sins because they do not have the Spirit of God working within them, and thus their works proceed from a wicked heart. David Hollaz writes:

> The upright works of unregenerate men, whether they be out of the church or have an external connection with it, which contribute to external order and the preservation of society, are civilly and morally to some extent good; but they are not good theologically and spiritually, nor do they please God; and therefore, in as much as they are destitute of the constituents of really good works, they are properly called splendid sins.[98]

This particular point of the reformers was attacked by the Roman church, which declared all who confess unbelievers' good works as sins to be anathema.[99] According to the opponents of the reformers, the external work, if in conformity with God's law, is not a sin, even if the person is unregenerate. In response to this claim, Quenstedt outlines three reasons why the good deeds of the unregenerate are indeed sins. First, these works are not done from faith, and whatever is not of faith is sin (Rom. 14:23). Second, the goal and object of one's deeds are sinful; they are performed, not for the sake of God, but for the sake of the self. Third, the person is different. The reality of regeneration changes an unrighteous person into a righteous one, and apart from this change, no deed can be called good.

## Conclusion

Luther's distinction between the two kinds of righteousness was not forgotten in the scholastic era. To the contrary, this theme has a prominent position in discussing the relationship between faith and works. Even if the explicit phrase "two kinds of righteousness" is not always utilized, there are

97. Ibid. III:44.

98. As cited in Weidner, *Pneumatology*, 186.

99. The Council of Trent as cited in Hoenecke, *Evangelical Lutheran Dogmatics* III:431.

several essential and prominent distinctions in historic Lutheran orthodox theology that correspond to Luther's twofold (and threefold) definition of righteousness. The two kinds of righteousness are described as the twofold effect of faith, whereby one is receptive before God and active in the world. This also corresponds to the distinction between justification and sanctification. In justification, one receives the imputed righteousness of Christ, and in sanctification one receives Christ's inherent righteousness. Hollaz has a similar distinction between monergistic operating grace and cooperating grace. There is also a distinction between the union of faith, wherein one is united with Christ as a mediator and receives his benefits, and divine indwelling, wherein the Christian is changed and performs good works. All of these kinds of inherent righteousness are placed in contradistinction to the civil righteousness of the unbeliever, thus substantiating a distinction between three kinds of righteousness.

This examination of the Lutheran scholastic theologians from the seventeenth to early twentieth centuries demonstrates that the contemporary treatment of this topic is consistent with Lutheran theological history. However, there are several important differences between some contemporary iterations of this teaching and that of older theologians. While Kolb and Arand argue that the two kinds of righteousness formulates an anthropological system, such a discussion is absent in the Lutheran scholastics. In the Lutheran dogmaticians, discussion of the two kinds of righteousness is treated within the *ordo salutis*, rather than as an aspect of theological anthropology. Also, the strict horizontal/vertical divide is absent in many of these older sources. The distinction of Brenz regarding the two hands of faith is similar to such a divide, but no theologians *limit* active righteousness to its horizontal dimensions. Pieper argues that good works are to be performed not only to benefit the neighbor, but also on account of the believer and God. It is true that active righteousness often has a horizontal *emphasis* in older Lutheran writers, but it is not exclusive of vertical dimensions. Finally, these older figures all admit that there are rewards in heaven for one's good deeds on earth. This contradicts Wingren's claim that good deeds are relevant *only* to the earth, and not to heaven. Though some differences remain between the Lutheran orthodox and contemporary figures, the two kinds of righteousness distinction itself is vindicated.

# Conclusion

## Two Kinds of Righteousness in Historic Lutheranism

It has been demonstrated that the theme of the two kinds of righteousness is not a new teaching, but is thoroughly consistent with historic Lutheran theology and with Scripture. Martin Luther expounded upon this teaching in his early writings "The Two Kinds of Righteousness" and "On Threefold Righteousness." Passive righteousness is received by faith, wherein God works for and in the believer. Active righteousness consists in the believer's good works. This theme arises throughout Luther's career, not simply in his early writings. His 1535 Galatians commentary claims that the uniqueness of Reformation theology consists in this distinction, which is lost in medieval scholasticism. The treatise *On Christian Liberty* is essentially an expansion of the theme of the two kinds of righteousness in the Christian's life. In one sense, the Christian is lord over all and servant of no one (passive righteousness), but in another sense he is servant of all (active righteousness). Luther also makes a distinction between the favor of God and the gift of God, which also roughly correspond to the two kinds of righteousness. The first is divine imputation, and the second divine indwelling.

One of the consistent themes throughout Luther's writings, as has been demonstrated, is union with Christ. For Luther, this union that occurs through faith is connected to both passive and active righteousness. Luther often conflates divine indwelling with justification, and thus can even talk about passive righteousness growing within the Christian. While passive righteousness is most often connected to divine imputation, it is occasionally used by Luther to refer to God's action in sanctification and the mystical union. The union that one has with Christ is the context for the great exchange, wherein Christ's righteousness is granted to the believer, and Christ takes the Christian's sin upon himself. This union is also connected to active righteousness, because this indwelling grows within the believer and causes good works of obedience.

The Lutheran confessional documents similarly expound upon this theme of the two kinds of righteousness. In his catechisms, Luther writes about the law of God not merely as that which demonstrates the reality of sin, but also as a guide for the Christian life. The life of the human creature *coram mundo* is guided by the divine law, even though one's obedience is irrelevant to justification before God. Good works are primarily a horizontal reality, performed for the good of others. The Lord's Prayer and the sacraments are not only related to passive righteousness, but additionally are means by which the Christian can begin to obey God's law, and then continues to do so increasingly.

The Augsburg Confession makes no explicit reference to the concept of the two kinds of righteousness, but both of these themes are present. In the Augustana, it is confessed that justification is received solely by faith, but that good works are also a necessary aspect of Christian existence. These good works of the Christian proceed from faith and thus differ from the civil righteousness of unbelievers. In his Apology, Melanchthon expounds upon these themes, using explicit two-kinds-of-righteousness terminology. Most often, Melanchthon speaks of the two kinds of righteousness in reference to passive righteousness and civic righteousness, or what he calls the "righteousness of reason." These two kinds of righteousness are both essential, but in different spheres. Through active righteousness, God preserves and governs the world; passive righteousness determines one's standing before God. Melanchthon also differentiates the active righteousness of the Christian from that of the unbeliever. Both perform externally beneficial acts, but the regenerate person does so from right motives and by the power of the Holy Spirit.

The Formula of Concord similarly uses explicit two-kinds-of-righteousness terminology. These two kinds of righteousness are imputed righteousness and indwelling righteousness. Imputation is a free gift received by faith alone, and what is imputed is an alien righteousness. The second kind of righteousness occurs by God's indwelling, wherein the Christian is renewed and performs good works. Both of these kinds of righteousness are essential for the Christian to receive, but for different functions. All who have passive righteousness will also have the indwelling Trinity and thus perform active deeds of righteousness in the world. The Formula of Concord also boldly confesses the third use of the law, contending that the believer's life in the world is guided by God's commandments. This law is not optional, but obedience is necessary. While arguing for the importance and necessity of good works, the Formula of Concord also guards against Major's proposition that "good works are necessary for salvation" by affirming that faith alone receives salvation.

The Lutheran confessional documents contain a fairly detailed treatment of both passive and active righteousness. Unlike some of Luther's writings, the Lutheran Confessions never identify passive righteousness with divine indwelling and the change which occurs in the believer by faith. Melanchthon only mentions justification in connection with passive righteousness in his Apology, and the Formula of Concord explicitly rejects the notion that passive righteousness is identical with the indwelling of God's being by which the Christian is renewed. In using the two kinds of righteousness in this manner, the reformers tighten Luther's definition of passive righteousness, utilizing a distinction more akin to Luther's discussion of Christ as grace and gift than his sermon "The Two Kinds of Righteousness."

The Lutheran theological tradition as developed after the Formula of Concord similarly continues to utilize the concept of the two kinds of righteousness. It was demonstrated that there are three primary ways in which this is done. First, many theologians, following Hollaz, distinguish between a twofold power of faith. Before God, faith is receptive of Christ's righteousness, and before the world, faith is active in love. Second, Lutheran theologians have continually distinguished between justification and sanctification. Justification includes the forgiveness of sins and the imputation of righteousness and is definitive of one's relationship with God. Sanctification regards the inherent righteousness of the Christian, wherein righteousness begins to be manifested in one's life. This is a progressive action of God and man, wherein man grows spiritually in holiness. These two aspects of the *ordo salutis* each have their distinctive spheres and must not be conflated with one another. Finally, some Lutherans have utilized the distinction between the *unio fidei formalis* and the *unio mystica*. Through the union of faith, one is united with Christ and thus appropriates his benefits. This is a passive-righteousness reality. Through the mystical union, the believer is changed through divine indwelling. The distinction between these two forms of union allow one to speak positively about the marriage union of faith spoken of by Luther without employing his confusing language of sanctification and indwelling as aspects of passive righteousness. In this way, the concern to distinguish indwelling from imputation is affirmed.

The Lutheran scholastic tradition affirms the essential elements of Luther's teaching on the two kinds of righteousness. It is confessed that there are two distinct forms of righteousness that all Christians have. These two kinds of righteousness are essential within their own spheres but must not be conflated with one another. Unlike Luther, the scholastics are more precise in their use of terminology and thus do not conflate renovation or divine indwelling with justification as Luther does in certain statements. Unfortunately, the Lutheran orthodox tradition also tends to neglect Luther's doctrine of vocation, and thus does not emphasize the horizontal reality of active righteousness. The scholastic tradition expounds consistently upon the elements of the two kinds of righteousness taught in the Lutheran Confessions. Like Luther in the Large Catechism, Lutheran theologians have argued that the law functions as a norm for the Christian life *coram mundo*. Commensurate with Melanchthon's teaching in the Apology, the Lutheran dogmaticians affirm the reality of civil righteousness, by which the unbeliever can perform outwardly righteous actions that benefit broader society. This civic righteousness is distinct from the active righteousness of the Christian in sanctification. The Christian's righteous deeds are performed out of faith and by the indwelling Holy Spirit. The Lutheran teaching of the mystical union is a legitimate expansion of the Formula's contention that the Holy Trinity dwells within Christians, conforming them to the image of God.

## Examining Contemporary Proposals

Now that the historic Lutheran teaching of the two kinds of righteousness has been explained, some important differences between this teaching and that of contemporary proponents of the two kinds of righteousness can be explicated. The basic contention of Wingren, Kolb, Arand, and Biermann is that there are two realms in which the Christian lives. All people have relationships with fellow creatures (*coram mundo*) and with God (*coram Deo*). Within these two realms, people function in different ways. Before God, one is passive and receives righteousness as a gift. Before the world, one is called to be active through works of love and service. This teaching is largely consistent with older teachings on the subject. Luther, particularly, speaks about justification as a vertical reality and sanctification as a horizontal reality. The Lutheran Confessions, especially in the Large Catechism, explain good works in such a manner. However, neither Melanchthon nor the Lutheran scholastics expound upon sanctification with a *sole* emphasis on the horizontal sphere. Pieper, for example, argues that good works are performed for the sake of God, the self, and the neighbor.[1] Though not ever serving as a basis for either justification or the preservation of faith, good works are performed for God as well as the neighbor.

The disparity between these approaches to active righteousness demonstrates a consistent divergence between contemporary iterations of the two kinds of righteousness and the scholastic tradition. One problem with contemporary approaches is that speaking of active righteousness as *only* a horizontal reality seems to negate the importance of the first table of the law. While Luther does, in his Large Catechism, expound upon the first three commandments as in some sense a *coram mundo* reality, they are not limited to such. It is certainly the case that one's attitude and piety toward God will affect how the neighbor is treated, but this does not negate a consistent vertical element in Christian living. While Wingren's strict division between faith as that which is aimed at God, and love as that which looks at the neighbor, is helpful, it is not exhaustive.[2] Scripture, as well as several Lutheran sources, also emphasize the love of God, and not simply so that the neighbor might be served. Gerhard, for example, explains love as a binding force between man and God, wherein love continually unites the Christian with God. He writes, "As your love is, so also you yourself are, because your love changes you. Love is the highest bond, because the one loving and the thing loved become one."[3] It is the "chariot of Elijah

---

1. "God commands Christians to lead a holy life 1) on His account. He does not want His children to serve sin and Satan. He wants them to serve Him, their rightful Lord, who has created them and then dearly purchased them by the blood of His Son. He redeemed them for this very purpose that they should lead a holy life . . . 2) Christians should perform good works on their own account. Sanctification and good works are to be for Christians the external testimony (*testimonium Spiritus Sancti externum*) of their state of grace and their possession of salvation . . . 3) Christians live a holy life on account of the world. By their holy life they should prove the truth of the Gospel to the unbelievers and thus induce them to hear the saving Word" (Pieper, *Christian Dogmatics* III:28–29).

2. The distinction between the twofold effects of faith demonstrates that faith also has a horizontal dimension.

3. Gerhard, *Sacred Meditations*, 48.

ascending to heaven."[4] This love has no place in justification, but allows one to grow in union with God. In the same manner he argues, "If you love the world, you become the world."[5] Walther echoes Gerhard on this: "The way of love is to be united with the beloved. If we love God, we will also be *one* spirit and heart with God."[6] This does not mean that one's relationship to God is ever *established* by obedience, but one's *experience* of union with God changes as faith grows.[7] I am not proposing that the common vertical/horizontal division in relation to the two kinds of righteousness needs to be discarded, but that it must not be viewed as an all-encompassing paradigm. It helpfully illustrates the horizontal reality of sanctification within the realm of God's creation, but it does not function comprehensively in explaining the importance of piety toward God.

There is need for a third category in the horizontal/vertical discussion. One cannot simply place love of God in the horizontal sphere—though the love of God will *always* necessarily result in horizontal action in the world. At the same time, piety toward God cannot be placed in the same *coram Deo* vertical category as passive righteousness. One must not expound upon love of God in such a way as to give the impression that one's relation to God is in any way dependent upon love toward God, rather than God's love toward man. One's piety can never increase God's love, but is a response to God's love. The proper category in which to place the first table of the law is of eucharistic sacrifice. The believer's love *for* God is always in thanksgiving for the love previously shown *by* God. This is why the preface (Ex 20:2) necessarily precedes the Decalogue. God's love toward man causes man's love toward God. Adding the category of thanksgiving does two important things: First, it allows for one to speak about the first table of the law without having to shift the focus from love of God to love of neighbor. Second, it ensures that the only context in which the first table is discussed is in view of passive righteousness, as it is done as a response to grace given. In this way, obedience to the first table of the law, like the second, is separated from any soteriological language.

4. Ibid.

5. Ibid.

6. Walther, *Selected Sermons*, 113.

7. Luther's marriage analogy is helpful here: After years of marriage, one is not "more married" to one's spouse, but that relationship grows more intimate and mature as the two parties learn more about one another.

While Wingren unfortunately neglects to discuss the proper place for the first table of the law in relation to one's life in the world, his work on vocation must be commended for revitalizing a theme of Luther's which was neglected in the post-Reformation era. The Lutheran scholastics in the seventeenth century did not explain Luther's doctrine of vocation as a separate locus, nor was it included in the topic of sanctification. The Lutheran tradition often echoes Melanchthon's approach to good works rather than Luther's, in which Melanchthon emphasizes good works generally, and especially piety toward God, without a consistent emphasis on the neighbor. On this point, Wingren's work should not be viewed as a contradictory approach to the scholastic one regarding the Christian life, but as a helpful expansion and further clarification of Luther's teaching on good works.

In the context of active righteousness, Kolb and Arand place a creational view of Christian living over and against theosis, arguing, "Luther opposed both the view of psychological transformation and the view of salvation by ontological transformation (both of which make sense only in a Platonic, spiritualizing frame of reference)."[8] Instead, "Luther rejoiced in his creatureliness. It is a great honor to be called a creature."[9] The theme of deification in Gerhard and treatments of the *unio mystica* thus seem to be negated by Kolb and Arand. Contrary to these two contemporary theologians, however, the historic Lutheran teaching of mystical union, or what I have labeled Christification, is not necessarily in contradistinction to the creational realm in which the Christian lives.[10] One's union with God does not take one *away* from creation, but brings one further *into* creation. The biblical model of theosis is cruciform. As God condescended into the world through the incarnation, so the Christian condescends to the world. Union with God grows, not simply in an otherworldly sphere, but within created reality. Christians model the incarnational life of Christ through serving one another in their vocations. Gerhard connects the *unio mystica* with life in the world: "God has communicated his entire self to you. Communicate also your entire self to your neighbor."[11] Wingren's emphasis on the nature

8. Kolb and Arand, *Genius of Luther's Theology*, 48.

9. Ibid., 38.

10. Kolb and Arand seem to limit union to the *unio fidei formalis*, noting, "The Christian is thus joined to Christ by a faith that clings to the Word and now accepts that Christ is totally responsible for us . . . Only in faith are Christ and a human being so joined together, so made one, that in God's judgment the human person participates in Christ's righteousness" (ibid., 46).

11. Gerhard, *Sacred Meditations*, 120.

of humanity as creatures and their service within the created realm is correct, and is not negated by Christification, but strengthened by it.

Kolb and Arand, in particular, argue that the two kinds of righteousness is not simply a model for understanding the distinction between faith and works, but constitutes a comprehensive theological anthropology. They contend that "Faith lies at the core of human existence."[12] Luther does not "consider the human person substantially" but instead "relationally and holistically."[13] One's identity as a creature is dependent, *coram Deo*, on the reality of the passivity of faith, and *coram mundo*, on active righteousness. This contention raises a number of theological problems. First, no previous Lutheran treatment of the two kinds of righteousness utilizes this distinction in such a way. Luther's sermon of that title is about the relationship between faith and works. There is no indication in that text that Luther is attempting to replace traditional philosophical anthropology with relational categories. Luther also does not discuss this in his Galatians commentary, his treatise *On Christian Liberty*, or his writing *Against Latomus*. While it is valid to discuss passive and active righteousness in terms of relation, there is no antithesis, in Luther, between relation and substance. The Lutheran Confessions, similarly, do not utilize the distinction in such a way. Melanchthon speaks about passive and active righteousness in terms of one's justification and life in the world before others. He never denounces substance-ontology, nor is this even under discussion in that particular section of the Apology.

The Formula of Concord likewise does not propound a new ontological system when outlining the two kinds of righteousness. It is discussed in Article III, which was a controversy surrounding the relationship between imputation and divine indwelling/renewal, not basic anthropology. Article I of the Formula of Concord is particularly helpful in establishing the anthropological convictions of the reformers. This article surrounds a controversy over Matthias Flacius's contention that sin was of the essence of the human creature following the fall. In contradistinction to this, the writers of the Formula contend that sin is not of the essence of the human creature, but an accident. If the reformers rejected a traditional Aristotelian model of being for a relational one, this article would have been the perfect place to use the distinction. Were that the case, the reformers would have contended that Flacius was mistaken because he employed false

---

12. Kolb, *Genius of Luther's Theology*, 38.

13. Ibid., 49.

metaphysical language that is in opposition to being as relation. Instead, the Formula expounds upon the use of the terms "substance" and "accident" in a traditional manner. They write:

> However, as far as the Latin words *substantia* and *accidens* are concerned, the churches should best be spared these terms in public preaching to the uninstructed, because such words are unfamiliar to the common people. If scholars want to use them among themselves or with others to whom they are not unfamiliar—as Eusebius, Ambrose, and especially Augustine, as well as other leading teachers of the church, did, more out of necessity to explain this teaching against the heretic—then we take them as an *immediata divisio* (that is, a distinction without a middle term), so that everything must be either *substantia*, that is, an independent essence, or *accidens*, that is, an incidental thing that has no essence in and of itself but rather exists in another independent essence and can be distinguished from it. (FC SD I.54)

While seeking to avoid philosophical abstraction in preaching, the reformers contended that such Patristic distinctions as substance and accident are valid. The human creature, therefore, according to the Lutheran Confessions, is not defined by relationships, but has a specific created substance. They further argue that "this is also an indisputable, incontrovertible axiom in theology, that each *substantia* or independent essence, insofar as it is a substance, is either God himself or a product and creation of God" (FC SD I.55). A substance is self-existing (though it only exists through God's creative word), and as a substance, human nature is self-existing. It is further declared to be an "incontrovertible truth" that "everything that exists is either a substance or an *accidens* (that is, either a self-subsistent essence or something contingent in such an essence)" (FC SD I.57). One who subscribes to the Lutheran Confessions therefore must affirm humanity as a self-existing substance.

The later Lutheran tradition similarly never expounds upon the two kinds of righteousness as an anthropological reality. The discussion surrounding passive and active righteousness is found solely within the context of soteriology, never metaphysics. Traditional Lutheran dogmatics textbooks include only the *imago Dei*, the state of integrity, and sin under the anthropology locus. Within the context of original sin, Flacius is often discussed, and the basic anthropological convictions of the Formula of Concord confirmed: man has a unique essence, and original sin is merely an accident. Quenstedt makes a helpful clarification here, however, that theology does not deal with the essence of man generally. Instead, he writes, "The subject of Theology is man, who fell into misery from his original happy state, and who is to be brought back to God and eternal salvation. The discussion here is not of man *as to his essence*, and as he is a creature . . . but as he is such or such a creature; and *in regard to his state*."[14] The theologian does not, then, seek to give a metaphysical explanation of the essence of man; however, this essence itself is affirmed as necessary to discuss man's state before and after the fall. It is possible that in the context of man after the fall, the two kinds of righteousness have a place in expounding upon man's place in the broader world theologically. However, this does not negate the importance of traditional categories of substance and accidents.

Another problem with the contention that the two kinds of righteousness define who man is, is that it simply does not account for the universal nature of the *imago Dei* and the value of all human life. If one's value before God is dependent upon the reception of passive righteousness, this would seem to have negative implications regarding those who are unconverted. Unbelievers, though not living passively before God as they are called to, still have value as human creatures. Their essential worth and humanness is not negated by the lack of passive righteousness. Similarly, the value of one in the world is not dependent solely upon active righteousness. The disabled individual, who has a complete inability to be active in the world, is still valuable before God and in the realm of God's creation. This would seem to be negated by the contention that one's status as human in the world is based solely on active righteousness, and before God by passive righteousness. The essential problem here is that there needs to be a distinction between being and relation. When the two are conflated, one's being is defined by one's relationships, and thus has no inherent value apart from these relationships. The two kinds of righteousness certainly have anthropological import, in that the distinction explains how one relates to God and to the world. However, there is still an essence of humanness, created by God, which stands behind these anthropological implications. Man's being is valuable in and of itself as a created substance of God.

## Ecumenical Implications

The teaching of the two kinds of righteousness has important implications within Lutheranism's relationship to other Christian traditions. Since the

14. Cited in Schmid, *Doctrinal Theology*, 220.

Reformation, the Lutheran church has been characterized as antinomian, lacking any grounds for the exercise of Christian piety and holiness. This accusation has been leveled not only by Roman Catholic opponents, but by other Reformation groups as well. Contemporary Reformed theologian John Frame, for example, writes in his *Systematic Theology* that "the prevailing view among Lutherans is that the third use is legitimate if it guides us by terrorizing us: making our sins vivid and driving us back to Christ again and again."[15] He further explains the Lutheran teaching on God's law, stating: "It is all bad news and no good news."[16] In his characterization, the third use of the law, for Lutherans, is simply the second use applied to Christians. It has no positive impact on Christian living. Similarly, the volume *Christian Spirituality: Five Views of Sanctification* contains an essay on the "Lutheran view" of sanctification written by Gerhard Forde. By including this essay, the implication given by the editors of this volume is that Forde's perspective on Christian living is representative of the broader Lutheran tradition. In this essay, often cited by theologians of other traditions, Forde limits God's sanctifying work to one's "getting used to justification." This approach to sanctification has limited ecumenical discussions with other various Christian traditions.

The distinction between the two kinds of righteousness helps to demonstrate important areas of agreement and discord among Lutheranism and other traditions. The distinction between active and passive righteousness demonstrates the essential differentiation between the Lutheran church and the Roman, but without negating the importance of the believer's active life of holiness. The Roman tradition is correct in emphasizing the necessity of good works, but it errs in conflating these works with justification. Instead, they belong to active righteousness. This also explains Lutheranism's relationship to Eastern Orthodox soteriology. The teaching of deification, in and of itself, is not problematic in a Lutheran perspective.[17] However, a conflation of theosis and passive righteousness obscures the chief article of justification.

There is also significant agreement between the Lutheran and Reformed traditions on this point. Calvin explicated the relationship between

15. Frame, *Systematic Theology*, 990.

16. Ibid.

17. This also depends on what type of deification, or theosis, one is speaking about. In my book *Christification*, I distinguish between the Patristic economical approach to theosis and the later Neo-Platonic view. It is the earlier, rather than the latter, which is consistent with Lutheran theology.

justification and sanctification by way of the *duplex gratia* (double grace). Karla Wubbenhorst demonstrates that Calvin's theology of justification and sanctification is rooted in his understanding of union with Christ. Calvin teaches that "the distinct graces of justification and sanctification not only are inseparable but also are established in us *at the same time* because, in Christ, we possess their common source."[18] Wubbenhorst refers to this as Calvin's *simul*. The Christian is simultaneously justified and sanctified. These two acts of God are distinct, and are connected through union with Christ. There is no causal relationship between the two actions of God, as justification does not effect sanctification.

For Calvin, faith is receptive in the same manner that Lutheran theologians argue. Wubbenhorst contends that faith is "a wholly receptive faculty."[19] Like Luther, Calvin argues that the believer's obedience to the law is irrelevant to justification. He writes that "the consciences of believers, in seeking assurance of their justification before God, should rise above and advance beyond the law, forgetting all righteousness."[20] However, Calvin is still a theologian of the law, emphasizing its positive function in the Christian life. He explains the relationship between justification and the law in the following words:

> Nor can any man rightly infer from this that the law is superfluous for believers, since it does not stop teaching and exhorting and urging them to good, even though before God's judgment seat it has no place in their consciences. For, inasmuch as these two things are very different, we must rightly and conscientiously distinguish them. The whole life of Christians ought to be a sort of practice of godliness, for we have been called to sanctification ... Here it is the function of the law, by warning men of their duty, to arouse them to a zeal for holiness and innocence. But where consciences are worried how to render God favorable, what they will reply, and with what assurance they will stand should they be called to his judgment, there we are not to reckon what the law requires, but Christ alone, who surpasses all perfection of the law, must be set forth as righteousness.[21]

18. Wubbenhorst, "Calvin's Doctrine of Justification," in McCormack, *Justification in Perspective*, 112.

19. Ibid., 108.

20. Calvin, *Institutes*, 834.

21. Calvin, *Institutes*, 835.

The law and gospel function within distinct spheres for Calvin, as they do in Luther. *Coram Deo*, the works of the Christian are irrelevant, as one is saved *sola fide*. The law is, however, both a guide and motivator for the Christian's life of holiness.

There are some notable differences between Calvin's view of the *duplex gratia* and the two kinds of righteousness. There is a prominence of sanctification which is not present in Luther. For Calvin, the third use of the law is its primary function, but for Lutherans, the second is. For Lutheran theologians, justification alone is the doctrine upon which the church stands or falls. For Calvin, justification and sanctification are equally important benefits of union with Christ. Another important distinction regards the relationship between active and passive righteousness. For Calvin, there is no causal relationship as both are received through the prior act of union with Christ. For Lutherans, however, justification is a cause of sanctification. Contemporary proposals argue that the nature of causation relates to God's effective speech-act, which does what it says. Older treatments, such as that of Adolf Hoenecke, find the connection in Christ himself. He writes that "through fellowship with Christ, that which happened to Christ for our justification is also to happen to us who are justified, namely, death and resurrection."[22] Like Calvin, Hoenecke maintains that Christ himself unites justification and sanctification, yet he still contends that justification is a cause of sanctification. Though important distinctions remain between the Lutheran and Reformed traditions, both are unified in their insistence on faith as the sole instrument of receiving forensic justification *coram Deo*, and the necessity of sanctified living *coram mundo*.

The distinction between the two kinds of righteousness helps to explain why Luther views the second use as the primary function of the law in opposition to Calvin. As explained above, the three uses of the law roughly correspond to the three kinds of righteousness. The first, or civil, use of the law corresponds to civic righteousness. This is the righteousness of the unbeliever whereby good and beneficial acts for the preservation of society can be performed. It is not, however, true Christian righteousness. The second use of the law corresponds to passive righteousness. These are both *coram Deo* realities. Before God, one is always condemned by God's law. This is the place for Melanchthon's principle *lex semper accusat*. Even the Christian's best actions, before God, are sinful. There is always some impure motive even when performing a good deed. Thus, every act of the Christian

---

22. Hoenecke, *Evangelical Lutheran Dogmatics* III:382.

*coram Deo* must be covered by the passive righteousness of Christ. One might then refer to the second use of the law as the *coram Deo* use of the law. The third use of the law corresponds to active righteousness. *Coram mundo*, the Christian has duties before others in the world. Here, one must learn how to treat one's neighbor, how to be faithful in one's family life, and how to live a life of piety. It is in this realm that, not the second, but the third use of the law is primary. The third use of the law is the *coram mundo* use of the law.

To understand the distinction between these two uses, one must not avoid explicating the law in its third use for fear of sounding Calvinistic rather than Lutheran. Rather, one must ask the question, which realm am I thinking of? If one is giving guidance to another Christian regarding how to live in this world, one should explicate God's law boldly as a helpful guide for the Christian in living out one's faith. When discussing one's relationship to God, however, the believer must always be reminded of the imperfection of his or her obedience and the daily failures of the Christian *coram Deo*. This explains why the second use is, for Luther, the law's primary use. It is not because the law does not also guide the believer in Christian obedience, or that this is not important. Rather, one's relationship to God is more important than one's relationship to fellow man. Passive righteousness is the foundation of active righteousness. Thus justification is always more central than sanctification, the second use more central than the third. That does not, however, negate the importance of Christian obedience. So long as one lives in the world, has the necessity to make decisions in life, and has duties and responsibilities, the law's third use is an absolute necessity.

## Two Kinds of Righteousness and Law and Gospel

Since the various professors at Concordia Seminary in St. Louis began publishing on the two kinds of righteousness, the theme has been prominent especially in online discussions about the role of justification, good works, and preaching. One of the primary contentions of those who oppose the utilization of the two-kinds-of-righteousness distinction is that such a distinction displaces law and gospel from its central position.[23] This has

23. Pastor and blogger Lincoln Winter writes, for example, "The latest trend that is sweeping the synod is called 'Two Kinds of Righteousness'. It is supposedly a very important theme throughout Luther, as demonstrated by the two sermons—one of which was written before the 95 Theses—and one lecture where it is found. Unfortunately, Luther

not been helped by the fact that Biermann has stated that the two kinds of righteousness is a "better paradigm" than law and gospel.[24] I contend, however, that these two important theological distinctions are not competing paradigms at all, but address different issues.

"Law and gospel" is essentially a description of how God speaks. God's words are promises (gospel) and commands (law). These two words must be distinguished in preaching, theological dialogue, and practice. Each is good and necessary, but the law and the gospel function in different manners. *Coram Deo*, law and gospel is the most helpful theological structure. Before God, Christians are shown their sin by God's law, and thus are prepared to hear the good news of the forgiveness of sins in Christ. However, Christians do not simply live before God. They also live in a world where they have to make decisions about how to live and how to treat other people. It is in this context that the two-kinds-of-righteousness distinction is essential. Here, these two ideas must be sharply distinguished. One's relationship to God is based in no way upon the human's active obedience, but upon the righteousness of God passively received. In contradistinction to this, one's relationship with others is not passive, but one must work for the benefit of one's neighbor. This distinction then is not answering the question of how God speaks (that is law and gospel), but how man relates to God (passive righteousness) and fellow-man (active righteousness). If these two paradigms address different issues, then there is no need to view them as contradictory.

Those who contend that the two-kinds-of-righteousness distinction somehow undermines law and gospel often point to the structure of preaching. It is said that the development of the two-kinds-of-righteousness paradigm is an attempt to replace a traditional law-gospel sermon structure with a passive-righteousness/active-righteousness sermon structure. This, however, is not really a helpful manner in which to look at preaching. Both

---

forgot to include it in his confessional writings. Melancthon may have hinted at it in the Augustana, but, then again, maybe he didn't. By the time the Formula of Concord was written, this 'very important' theology of Luther was apparently lost. Fortunately, a doctoral student about ten years ago picked up on it. And now, some professors at our seminaries are encouraging their students to use this as a paradigm for understanding scripture, as opposed to, say, 'Law and Gospel.' Because apparently, the constant obvious references to Law and Gospel throughout the confessions are really just Luther wishing he wrote more about 2KR (Like all things hip and cool, it has its own acronym)" (Winter, "Law and Gospel Are Good Enough For Me").

24. Biermann has given a talk at several locations titled "Two Kinds of Righteousness: A Better Paradigm."

law and gospel and the two kinds of righteousness need to be *distinguished* in preaching, but neither needs to provide the sole *structure* of each sermon. In historic Lutheran preaching, the message was not divided into 1. *Law, and* 2. *Gospel*.[25] This is a modern trend that seems to identify more with existential Lutheranism than Lutheran orthodoxy. Instead of imposing a preconceived structure on each text, whether that is law and gospel or the two kinds of righteousness, the pastor should preach according to whatever text he is given. Sometimes that is going to be a straightforward law-gospel sermon, but other times it will include a heavy amount of exhortation to serve one's neighbor in obedience to God's will, though always in view of the gospel.

Both the law-gospel and the passive/active-righteousness distinctions are essential for the Lutheran pastor, and neither needs to be neglected in favor of the other. Law and gospel remind us that Christians always fall short of God's will and are saved solely by God's grace. The two kinds of righteousness remind God's people that they cannot work to merit God's favor or love, but that righteousness is given freely, and that they are called to live holy lives in the world for the sake of others.

## Navigating the Path between Legalism and Antinomianism

From its inception, the church has fought against two opposing errors: legalism and antinomianism. On the one hand, Christians have been tempted to emphasize the law over the gospel, relegating the Christian life to a series of rules and regulations. This has blatant forms, wherein it is contended that salvation is earned by human obedience, but there are also more subtle forms of this error. In the quest for assurance, some have pointed Christians inward for signs of true conversion in opposition to possible false conversion. On the other hand, there is the error of antinomianism, or animosity toward God's law. This comes in extreme forms, such as in the theology of Agricola, who argued that the law had no relevance for Christian preaching, and in more subtle forms, wherein the reality of Christian obedience is ignored. The distinction between the two kinds of righteousness guards against both of these errors.

"How can I find a gracious God?" was the central question Luther asked that began the Reformation. The primary concern for Luther, against

---

25. Look, for example, at the sermons of C.F.W. Walther in Walther, *Selected Sermons*.

legalistic preaching and teaching, was for personal assurance. The distinction between the two kinds of righteousness affirms that one's relationship to God is based solely on the passivity of faith. One cannot earn righteousness *coram Deo*. It is pure reception. With this idea in mind, therefore, one need not look to outward good deeds to gain assurance of salvation. If justification arises solely by faith, then assurance can be gained without regard for one's works in the *coram mundo* sphere. Though good works in the *coram mundo* realm are a necessary result of faith and are testaments to the reality of faith and regeneration, Christian obedience can *never* function as the basis for Christian assurance. Instead, assurance is to be found in the *gratia universalis* (universal grace) and the righteousness granted by God through the means of word and sacrament. The *coram Deo/coram mundo* distinction guards against unhelpful phraseology such as "good works are necessary for salvation," or "good works retain salvation" by rejecting the efficacy of good deeds *coram Deo*. The sinner struggling with assurance should not be pointed to active righteousness, but solely to the righteousness of God received in faith.

Luther's distinction between the two kinds of righteousness also guards against the error of antinomianism. One could be tempted to think, due to the reality of justification *sola fide*, that good works are irrelevant in the Christian life. Rather than negating the necessity of good works, the distinction between the two kinds of righteousness places good works within their proper sphere. The Christian no longer performs good works to gain, retain, or prove his salvation. Instead, these works can be done in true freedom, with no other motive than to serve the neighbor and please God by following his will. With this distinction in mind, Christian preachers should not diminish the importance of good works, but instead proclaim them boldly. As long as the Christian lives in the flesh within the world, he is called to obey God and serve those around him within his various vocations.

This distinction is extremely helpful pastorally. The teaching of the twofold righteousness is not merely an academic one, but is immensely practical. Lutheran pastors sometimes feel constricted in preaching on specific good works for fear that doing so will result in legalism and displacing the central article of justification. With this distinction, however, the pastor is given the tools whereby the Christian's good works can be helpfully explained in the Christian life while retaining the central reality of justification *coram Deo*. Just as Luther and other Lutheran fathers were not timid in proclaiming the importance and necessity of good deeds from the pulpit, so should the pastors of the Lutheran church today do, so long as they continually emphasize the sole saving efficacy of faith before God.

Though passive righteousness is the primary context in which the pastor is placed in relation to the congregation, he is also called to equip and encourage the congregants unto lives of active righteousness in the world. His central message is justification, but secondary is sanctification. The pastor is not primarily placed in his office to be a motivator to the congregation, but he must teach people that the passive righteousness received in faith always leads to active righteousness of love out in the world. An understanding of active righteousness solves several common congregational issues in Lutheran churches. Understanding active righteousness will give the people a realization that the Christian faith affects all areas of their lives, not simply Sunday mornings. It also puts the mission of the church in reaching out with works of love and service in a proper and helpful context. Finally, teaching active righteousness helps to build the understanding of the church as a community.

It is a constant danger in the Lutheran church for people to assume that the Christian faith is only relevant to their lives on Sunday mornings. Because of the emphasis the church places on the forgiveness of sins, there are many congregants who go to church Sunday mornings to receive their forgiveness for the week in the sacrament and then leave the service ready to ignore their Christian faith until the next Sunday morning. They simply have no place for the Christian life in their daily activities, because what is talked about in church is the relationship one has with God, but during the week, one has to focus on one's relationship with fellow human beings. It is easy for one to assume that the Christian faith is not relevant to ordinary life.

An understanding of active righteousness, especially in the context of vocation, will give the congregants a manner in which they can connect the forgiveness received on Sunday to their active lives in their jobs, families, and communities. Luther argued that the faith has a profound impact on daily living, because God has called Christians into various vocations in the world. These vocations are opportunities to serve one's neighbors, as God uses people as his own hands to serve the world. Pastors need to teach on this doctrine of vocation on a regular basis. The congregants need to understand that the Bible speaks not only to their relationship with God in the church, but to their place in the broader community also. The grace of

God gives one motivation to serve the neighbor in one's job and also within family life. Paul gives extensive exhortations to husbands, wives, parents, and children (Eph 5:21–6:9). This need not happen in the context of motivational speeches during the Sunday service on how to be a good father or husband. But as does Paul, the pastor can give such admonitions in light of the free forgiveness of sins that comes through the gospel.

Luther's doctrine of active righteousness does not only affect the individual's relationship to one's family, co-workers, and neighbors, but it also informs the function of the church. The church's primary mission is to proclaim the gospel, but the church also must actively serve the community. It does this through providing for the spiritual and physical needs of others. The church must be active in bringing the gospel to the broader culture, proclaiming the forgiveness of sins to those who do not yet believe it; it also ought to be active in providing the community with various needs that is has.

Works of love and service are also intimately connected to the task of the church. It is incumbent upon the church to provide for not only the spiritual, but also the physical needs of the community. This can be done in several different ways. Some churches run soup kitchens or food banks, whereas others donate gifts to the poor in some other manner. What often happens is that the church views its relationship to the community as one of reception. The community is viewed as a resource which the church should draw on to raise funds. This is why fundraising events are the norm. However, when it is understood that one's relationship to the world is not passive but active, then the church will begin to see itself as a resource to the community rather than vice versa. It is here that actual outreach can begin. There is often a failure of the church in recognizing itself as a community of believers. People sometimes see only the vertical dimension of the service while failing to understand the importance of Christian fellowship on the horizontal level. They go to church for the purpose of hearing the sermon and receiving the sacraments, and then they leave the doors of the church without any further interaction with those in the congregation on Sunday morning. When this happens, the fellowship tears itself apart, and it hampers visitors from returning to the church. When people visit a church, they are often looking for fulfillment of both the vertical and horizontal relationships in their lives. They want good preaching, but they also want some sense of community and fellowship. Lacking this aspect of horizontal righteousness will ruin the local church and opportunities for outreach.

The New Testament is very concerned about the nature of the relationships developed between fellow believers in the congregation. Paul urges the Galatians to "do good to all men, and especially to those who are of the household of faith" (Gal 6:10). This informs us that the Christian's duty horizontally is not only outward toward the unbelieving world, but also, and even principally, to those who are in the church. This is why Paul spent time tackling the divisions that occurred within the Corinthian church, admonishing, "I appeal to you, brethren, by the name of our Lord Jesus Christ, that all of you agree and that there be no dissensions among you, but that you be united in the same mind and the same judgment" (1 Cor 1:10). This lack of horizontal fellowship between Christians almost ruined that congregation. At the inception of the church this intimate fellowship was experienced perhaps more profoundly than ever in the church's history. Luke writes, "Now the company of those who believed were of one heart and soul, and no one said that any of the things which he possessed was his own, but they had everything in common" (Acts 4:32). It is apparent that the unity and fellowship of believers is a central concern of the New Testament.

The moral life of the Christian in the world should be expressed not only in sermons, but in regular catechesis. When teaching a Bible study, a pastor will come to certain passages that expound upon particular moral behaviors that are expected of Christian people. Rather than skipping over these texts, or *only* emphasizing the fact that Christians fail to obey these commandments, the pastor should apply these imperatives to the practical and individual lives of congregants, so that they are instructed not only in doctrine, but in holiness. Similarly, confirmation classes and new-member courses should employ moral catechesis alongside of theological training.

The distinction between active and passive righteousness is not a theological abstraction, but is immensely helpful in practical pastoral ministry. On the one hand, passive righteousness helps the believers to understand who they are in Christ. A proper understanding of the righteousness that comes from God by imputation guards against contemporary problems in the church such as pragmatism, moralism, and emotionalism. On the other hand, active righteous is a necessary teaching to instruct the church in its manner of acting in the broader world. A proper understanding of this second type of righteousness helps the church to understand its mission in giving to the spiritual and physical needs of the outside world, as well as encouraging fellowship within the body of Christ.

# Conclusion

## Concluding Reflections

The rise of the two-kinds-of-righteousness distinction in contemporary Lutheranism has been a beneficial move within the church. Through this distinction, one can boldly speak against antinomianism while still retaining the centrality of justification *coram Deo*. Such a distinction is valuable, not only for the Lutheran church, but the entire Christian world. Along with avoiding antinomianism, such a distinction would help non-Lutheran churches to be careful in their terminology regarding salvation and the purpose of good works within the life of the Christian. This distinction helps to assure troubled consciences that their sins are forgiven solely on account of Christ's righteousness passively received; it also helps preachers to place faith and good works within their proper contexts.

Ultimately this distinction is one that needs to be played out within parish life. Active and passive righteousness are not purely theoretical theological categories, but important realities within which all people live. God's people live right at the center of two realities. We are constantly engaged in two different spheres. Every action we take is done before God and within the created world. The two-kinds-of-righteousness distinction helps us to live in light of these actions so that we better understand who we are as God's creatures and what the world is in which we live.

The distinction between the two kinds of righteousness deserves further development. There are a number of different areas of discourse in which this distinction can be applied. This is true not only of distinctly theological disciplines, but also in other areas of life and study in which the Christian is called to be active in the world. It is my hope that scholars will continue to develop this theme and further explore its history within Lutheran theology, and more importantly, its exegetical basis. I also hope that this theme will continue to be explored in popular works aimed at laity, and most critically, from the pulpit.

# Appendix

# Two Kinds of Righteousness in Scripture

It has been firmly established that the theme of the two kinds of righteousness is inherent within the Lutheran tradition. In this appendix, the biblical theme of these two kinds of righteousness will be explored, demonstrating that both kinds of righteousness are thoroughly biblical, as is a form of the *coram Deo/coram mundo* distinction advocated by contemporary proponents of the two kinds of righteousness. Due to the nature of this work, this article will only serve as a brief overview of the biblical nature of the two kinds of righteousness, rather than as an extensive exegetical treatment.

## Before the Fall

The two kinds of righteousness are present from the creation narrative of Genesis 1 and 2. God's creation of man and woman is an act of grace. God breathed life into Adam as he created him from the dust of the earth. Adam had no role in establishing his own being and identity in the world. This was a result of pure gift. As we expound upon this theme, some clear differences emerge between a Lutheran and Reformed perspective on man's prelapsarian state.

In traditional Reformed federal theology, a distinction is made between a covenant of works and a covenant of grace.[1] In a covenant of works,

---

1. There are three covenants in Reformed theology: the covenant of redemption, the covenant of works, and the covenant of grace (Horton, *Christian Faith*, 45).

God grants blessings based on obedience and punishes disobedience. In a covenant of grace, God gives blessings unconditionally. It is argued that before the fall, Adam was placed in a covenant of works with God. In order to gain life, Adam had to be obedient to God's will.[2] In the prelapsarian state, therefore, Adam could merit his standing before his Creator. Wilhelmus Brakel explains: "The covenant of works was an agreement between God and the human race as represented in Adam, in which God promised eternal life upon condition of obedience, and threatened eternal death upon disobedience. Adam accepted both this promise and this condition."[3] In federal theology, it is only after the fall that God instituted the covenant of grace in Genesis 3:15. This covenant of grace extends throughout the Abrahamic, Davidic, and New covenants. The Mosaic covenant is sometimes described as a covenant of grace, but by others is explained as a republication of the covenant of works.[4] In this manner of theologizing, there is an immense difference between God's manner of relating to man before and after the fall. In this perspective, grace, and consequently passive righteousness, can only properly be spoken of as a post-fall reality.

I contend, in contrast the Reformed view, that before the fall, man still existed in the same two basic kinds of relationships that he does today: with God, and with the world. These two relationships function in accordance with the two-kinds-of-righteousness paradigm. Even in Eden, Adam and Eve lived by grace before God and by works before the world. In the Calvinistic approach to the covenant of works, *both* of these relationships are based on active righteousness. Adam's standing in the world *and before God* were based upon his own personal obedience. In Luther's view, however, grace is connected to creation itself. In his exposition of the first article of the Creed, Luther writes:

> I believe that God has made me and all creatures; that He has given me my body and soul, eyes, ears, and all my limbs, my reason, and all my senses, and still preserves them; in addition thereto, clothing and shoes, meat and drink, house and homestead, wife and children, fields, cattle, and all my goods; that He provides me richly and daily with all that I need to support this body and life,

2. "The first covenant made with man was a covenant of works, wherein life was promised to Adam; and in him to his posterity, upon condition of perfect and personal obedience" (WCF 7.2).

3. Cited in Bolt, "Why the Covenant of Works," 173.

4. For the "covenant of works" view of the Mosaic covenant, see Horton, *Covenant and Salvation*, 11–36. For the opposing perspective, see Elam, *Merit and Moses*.

protects me from all danger, and guards me and preserves me from all evil; and all this out of pure, fatherly, divine goodness and mercy, without any merit or worthiness in me; for all which I owe it to Him to thank, praise, serve, and obey Him. This is most certainly true. (SC II.1)

The very act of creation, for Luther, is a work of grace. God's way of working with man has always been one of grace, from creation through redemption. This demonstrates that the two-kinds-of-righteousness distinction is not only a post-fall reality, but relates to the very essence of God's character and man's created purpose.

In the Genesis narrative, God gives Adam everything he needs for his bodily life as a free gift. God gives Adam his spirit by breathing into him. He gives him land to take care of, food to eat, and a wife to love. God fellowships with man face to face. There is no indication that man, by his works, could gain such a relationship, or continue such a relationship, on the basis of his own deeds. Throughout the narrative, God is pictured as a giver of gifts to his creation, not as a lawgiver placing strict demands before Adam in order that he might merit confirmation in righteousness.

The commands God gives to Adam, then, are not demands of righteousness *coram Deo*, but fatherly instructions about how he is to live in the created realm. All of the various laws given before the fall are related to man's particular place within creation. They are all references to man's relationship to fellow creatures. The first commandment given to Adam and Eve in the creation account is as follows: "Be fruitful and multiply and fill the earth and subdue it and have dominion over the fish of the sea and over the birds of the heavens and over every living thing that moves on the earth" (Gen 1:28). This text, sometimes called the "cultural mandate," explains the precise role of God's law prior to sin. It is a guide for man and woman so that they might fulfill their proper roles within their created sphere. Serving under God, the great King, they are called to function as a creature king and queen, ruling over all of the things of the earth.[5] Note that immediately following this commandment, God reminds them that he is the one who provides for all needs necessary to function *coram mundo*: "Behold, I have given you every plant yielding seed that is on the face of all the earth, and every tree with seed in its fruit" (Gen 1:29). The same pattern emerges: God is pictured as a loving provider, and gives man, apart from

---

5. Meredith Kline rightly expounds upon this idea of man serving under God, the great King; see Kline, *Kingdom Prologue*, 43–45.

works, everything he needs for body and life. Man then takes these gifts and uses them to serve creation in accordance with God's law.

The second chapter of Genesis contains a similar pattern of man's proper functioning in the prelapsarian state. There are two specific trees mentioned in the Edenic narrative: the tree of life and the tree of the knowledge of good and evil. In light of its place elsewhere in Scripture (Rev 2:7, 22:2), it is apparent that the tree of life is connected with eschatological life. This tree is sacramental in nature. By partaking of this fruit, man received from God the sustenance of his spiritual life. It is clear in the text that God allowed man to partake of this tree, because Adam is told that he may eat of "every tree in the garden" (Gen 2:16), excepting the tree of the knowledge of good and evil. Adam's life would be sustained, then, by the tree of life, which appears as the first means of grace. Again, there is no indication that Adam needed to work in order to partake of the tree of life. Instead, it is because of the life that he had been graciously given by God that he was given his creaturely duties to work and keep the garden (Gen 2:15) and to name the animals (Gen 2:20).

Never in the text of Genesis is Adam told that he will gain life by his obedience. He is only told that he could *lose* life by his disobedience. Adam was already in God's favor by creation. He did not need to earn that favor. But God did grant Adam a choice, so that he could walk away from God's grace, bringing death upon himself and his descendants. There is an implicit assumption in Reformed arguments that because Adam could do something to *lose* life, he could conversely perform some work to *gain* life. Such an assumption is unwarranted, and is not defensible from the text of Genesis. Instead, man's passive relationship to God and active relationship to the world are essential to who he is created to be, not simply a post-fall situation.

The structure of active and passive righteousness existed even prior to the fall. God created Adam by grace and provided for all of his bodily needs. Adam lived before God by receiving his gifts and offering thanksgiving. Yet, these gifts passively given were then provided so that Adam might be active in his life, not *coram Deo*, but *coram mundo*. The gifts of life and sustenance given freely by God were to be used by Adam to serve creation.

## The Post-Fall World

After the fall, God still chose to live within the same type of relationship to his (now fallen) creation. Rather than giving Adam and Eve their just punishment of eternal death, he promised them that a Messiah would come to crush the head of the serpent (Gen 3:15). He also covered their shame and nakedness (Gen 3:21). Though man's relationship to God remained intact after the fall, men and women were given specific punishments which must be faced in this life. The woman would have pain in childbearing (Gen 3:16), and the man would have difficulty performing his God-given tasks (Gen 3:17–19). It is significant that both of these curses relate to the particular commandments God gave to each sex prior to the fall. Man's role *coram mundo* was to till the earth. Woman's role *coram mundo* was to bear children. Thus we see here a clear distinction between man's life *coram Deo* and *coram mundo*. God's relationship to his creation remains one of pure grace, but there are legitimate temporal consequences for sin *coram mundo*.

The relationship that God established with man through passive righteousness remains throughout the Old Testament. In the story of Abraham, the author writes about a covenant made, in which God will fulfill the necessary conditions. The call of Abraham in Genesis 12 is a result of pure grace. God simply tells Abraham that he will make him great (Gen 12:1). There is no indication that Abraham was chosen based on any righteousness within him. Abraham simply receives that promise in faith, and by that faith, Abraham is declared righteous (Gen 15:6). This promise is then ratified by a covenant. God puts Abraham to sleep, and in the form of a fire pot and flaming torch, God passes through three sacrificed animals.[6] The implication in this text is that God is the one who will fulfill the necessary obligations of this covenant, not Abraham. Just as the animals were sacrificed, God himself would give his Son's life as an atonement, so that the Abrahamic promise might be fulfilled. This is particularly significant because, as Roehrs notes, "The covenant with Abraham . . . was not merely the first [covenant] but also preeminent and permanent. Its promise underlies

---

6. Meredith Kline expounds upon this idea in relation to ancient Hittite suzerainty vassal treaties. In one of these ancient treaties, a great king would make a covenant with a lesser king. One would "cut a covenant," which was a ceremony in which the lesser king would walk through the bodies of sacrificed animals. In doing this, they made an agreement that the lesser king would obey the covenant stipulations, and if he failed to do so, he would be cut apart like the animal. Since God (the suzerain) is the one who walked through the pieces, he took upon himself the curses of Abraham's disobedience to the covenant (Kline, *Kingdom Prologue*, 292–355).

all God's deeds for and through Israel."[7] Thus, if the Abrahamic promise is based upon pure passive righteousness, then so is the entire history of Israel.

## The Ten Commandments

The story of the Exodus continues this theme of divine initiative in salvation and man's receptivity of God's gifts. In the narrative, God raises up a Messiah figure (a type of Christ), Moses, who led the people of Israel out of captivity. He does this through the ten plagues sent to Egypt, the Passover sacrifice, and the crossing of the Red Sea. God continues to establish himself as the redeemer, and one who redeems regardless of the sins of those whom he is rescuing.

It is precisely in this context that the Ten Commandments are given to the nation of Israel. God has already established his people by grace through the promises given to Abraham and Moses. The commandments, then, are given *in light of the gospel*. This is why the Ten Commandments begin with the prologue "I am the Lord your God, who brought you out of the land of Egypt, out of the house of slavery" (Ex 20:1). The words that follow this declaration are a description of how a redeemed people is supposed to live. Dean Wenthe argues that many within the Reformation tradition have unfortunately removed the divine commandments from their narrative context. In doing so, the preceding redemption God granted to the Israelites is lost, and the Ten Commandments are viewed purely in a second-use context. In contrast to this, Wenthe contends that the law is "a wonderful guide to the man or woman who is in Christ."[8] In other words, the Ten Commandments are an exposition of *coram mundo* righteousness in view of the fact that one's *coram Deo* righteousness has already been established by grace. They are given in a third-use context.

The Mosaic covenant is distinct from the promise given to Abraham. Though the Abrahamic promise underlies much of the narrative surrounding Moses, the covenant itself includes curses and blessings based on one's *coram mundo* righteousness. While the Abrahamic promise is ratified by God while Abraham is asleep, the Mosaic covenant includes an aspect of human fulfillment. After Moses explained all of the various commandments that God had given the nation of Israel, the people declared, "All the

7. Roehrs, *Survey*, 35.
8. Wenthe, "Torah Story," 27.

words that the Lord has spoken we will do" (Ex 24:3). God then includes very specific blessings and curses based upon the obedience of the people in Deuteronomy 28. This does not mean that the Israelites were in any way saved by such obedience. However, there are temporal consequences to one's *coram mundo* actions. Revere Franklin Weidner writes:

> [God's] judgements have a fixed end, and therefore are always in measure, as is taught in the beautiful parable in Isa. 28:23–29. They are so executed that Israel is brought back to God, and the perfecting of God's kingdom is secured. Israel is not annihilated in the judgment . . . Thus, in spite of man's sin and faithlessness, the realization of the divine decree, the perfecting of the people of God, is firmly based on God's faithfulness and mercy.[9]

The interplay between these two types of relationships is clear in the lives of Daniel, Jeremiah, and other faithful Jews during the exile. These prophets had to suffer the temporal consequences of the sins of the nation to which they belonged. Thus they suffered *coram mundo*. Yet it is abundantly clear that they had faith in Yahweh and were righteous before God due to their trust in God's promises. The same individual lives in a right relationship to God and faces temporal consequences of sin. Ultimately, even the goal of God's punishment for sin is redemption and restoration.

The covenant with Moses is not, however, purely a guide for *coram mundo* living. In the Mosaic administration, God continues to show his unconditional grace in saving sinners. Walter Robert Roehr notes that the "covenant would never be based on merit. It would remain His instrument of grace to a people that had not and never would deserve what He had bound and pledged Himself to give in the promises to the patriarchs and to the fathers at Sinai."[10] This is clear in that the Mosaic administration included within it provisions for sin in the sacrificial system. There were a number of typological elements in Israelite religion, such as the sacrifices, the scapegoat, and the priesthood, which served as a constant reminder that salvation was a result of God's forgiveness and human reception, not of works.

The passive righteousness of faith is a consistent Old Testament theme. Every time the Abrahamic and Davidic promises are mentioned by the prophets, these are mentions of the righteousness that God grants freely, apart from works. Each of the Psalms of confession and repentance (Pss 32,

---

9. Weidner, *Biblical Theology of the Old Testament*, 129.

10. Roehr, *Survey of Covenant History*, 83.

51, etc.) is similarly a testimony to God's gracious attitude toward sinners. This theme is interwoven with a variety of instructions given to the people of Israel. The book of Proverbs, for example, is a text about *coram mundo* righteousness. Proverbs consistently speaks of the "fear of God" as the beginning of the wisdom (e.g., Prov 1:7), which the author expounds upon. Thus, Proverbs is not primarily dealing with the "second use" of the law, but instead serves as a description of how faith in Yahweh demonstrates itself in living with wisdom. The Babylonian exile serves as an example of *coram mundo* consequences for sin, and the restoration is an example of God's unrelenting grace. Both active and passive righteousness are found throughout the Old Testament texts.

## Passive Righteousness in the Pauline Epistles

Luther's explanation of the two kinds of righteousness is essentially an extrapolation of Pauline theology. Thus, Paul's epistles are the most important biblical texts within this discussion. In Paul's theology, salvation is the result of grace apart from works. Good deeds are the inevitable fruit of faith and are used to serve the neighbor. The three epistles which are utilized in the discussion surrounding justification the most extensively are Romans, Galatians, and Ephesians. In each of these three letters, Paul explains the proper use of God's law in bringing one to repentance, the nature of salvation, and the necessity of good deeds following regeneration. Since much ink has been spilled over all of these texts, this will be a simple, short overview of the Pauline text, and extensive discussions are to be found elsewhere.

The book of Romans is central to the theology of the Reformation.[11] In the beginning of this book, Paul gives an indictment against all of humankind for rejecting God's righteousness and seeking to establish their own. He discusses the reality of God's wrath due to human sin and wickedness (Rom 1:18). Through creation, all people are held accountable to God

11. Martin Luther said of the letter, "This epistle is the very heart and center of the New Testament and the purest and clearest Gospel. It well deserves to be memorized word for word by every Christian man . . . Thus we find in the epistle all that a Christian ought to know, and that in great abundance, namely, what the Law is, what the Gospel is, what sin and punishment are, what grace, faith, righteousness, Christ, God, good works, love, hope, and the cross are, and what our attitude toward all men ought to be, toward saints and sinners, the strong and the weak, friend and foe, and toward ourselves" (cited in Franzmann, *Word of the Lord*, 118).

and are responsible to offer him worship (Rom 1:20). The Gentiles reject worship of the true God, and instead worship those things which God has created, rather than the Creator himself (Rom 1:23). This results in a perversion of God's created order, wherein men and women exchange their natural relations with one another for those of the same sex (Rom 1:27). Paul then indicts the Jews for similarly rejecting God while simultaneously bragging in their ethnic heritage (Rom 2:17–24). Paul concludes that all people are found guilty *coram Deo* by the law of God (Rom 3:19). This is because the purpose of the law was never to bring about righteousness, but to shut every mouth, that all people might come to a realization about their sinful and condemned state (Rom 3:20). In this section, it is apparent that the second use of the law is its *coram Deo* use. There is none who has not sinned, and righteousness before God cannot be attained by human performance.

Following this indictment, Paul begins to speak about the righteousness of God. This righteousness is not attained through obedience to God's law (Rom 3:28); it is received, instead, through faith (Rom 3:22). All who believe, both Jews and Gentiles, receive this righteousness as a gift of God. This righteousness arises through Christ's death, whereby one is redeemed (Rom 3:24–25). Even those who are ungodly are considered righteous through faith (Rom 4:5), just as Abraham and David received righteousness by the means of faith (Rom 4:1–8).

One might concede all of these points, but contend that it is only at the *beginning* of the life of faith that such righteousness is credited. Perhaps after such a point, the third use of the law becomes predominant, and one's active righteousness determines the continual nature of the *coram Deo* relationship. This contention is contradicted by two points within the text. First, neither of Paul's examples of justification by faith from the Old Testament are texts referring to the beginning of the life of faith. Paul first cites the example of Abraham in Genesis 15, wherein he is said to be righteous for believing in God's promises.[12] This particular text arises three chapters after the initial call of Abraham in Genesis 12. In other words, Abraham had been following God for quite some time, and yet his relationship to God was *still* determined by faith alone. Note also that Paul uses Abraham as an example of God justifying the *ungodly* (Rom 4:5). In some sense, even obedient and believing Abraham was considered "ungodly." His standing before God was not as a wage given to one working, but as a gift (Rom

---

12. I give a more extensive discussion of this issue in Cooper, *Great Divide*, 172–73.

4:4). Similarly, David's confession of sin and repentance is an example of justification of the ungodly (Rom 4:7–8). *Coram Deo*, both David and Abraham are *simul iustus et peccator*, as are all with faith in Christ. Second, Paul explicitly speaks about the condemnatory nature of God's law in the present tense, as a description of his present experience (Rom 7:14–25). This paradoxical reality of sin and righteousness in the Christian life will only come to an end when one is "delivered from this body of death" at the eschaton (Rom 7:24).[13]

Paul's letter to the Galatians similarly discusses the nature of faith and works in the Christian life and their relationship to saving righteousness. When opening this letter, Paul reminds the Galatians that their salvation is due to Christ's death, through which we are delivered (Gal 1:4). He then argues that preaching another gospel is anathema (Gal 1:8). This "other gospel" is one which teaches salvation by works of the law. In contrast to this, Paul argues that righteousness arises not by law, but by faith (Gal 3:6). The law, in contrast to faith, promises life to all who put forth effort in obedience (Gal 3:12). All people who disobey God's law are under its curse— and no one obeys God's law (Gal 3:10).[14] Christ came so that this curse might be placed upon him rather than the human race (Gal 3:13). Paul explicitly distinguishes between law and gospel by differentiating God's commandments and his promises (Gal 3:18).[15] Before God, it is only the promise which saves that is received by faith. The purpose of the law was not to save, but instead to condemn all people as sinners (Gal 3:22). Like Romans, the book of Galatians teaches that the role of the law *coram Deo* is to convict the world of sin, and that righteousness is received by faith in God's promises.

There are a number of different ways in the book of Ephesians by which passive righteousness is explained. Paul opens this epistle by describing the reality of divine election. God initiated the salvation of his elect even prior to the act of creation (Eph 1:4). This election includes the Christian

13. For a book-length argument that Romans 7 is descriptive of the present Christian experience, see Middendorf, *I in the Storm*.

14. The proponents of the New Perspective on Paul, as well as some Federal Vision writers, argue that the law does not, in fact, require perfect obedience. A helpful discussion of these issues can be found in Silva, "Faith Versus Works of Law in Galatians," in *Variegated Nomism*, II:217–48.

15. Though many contemporary interpreters have rejected a historic law-gospel distinction as Pauline, Stephen Westerholm gives a masterful defense of the traditional view in *Lutheran Paul*, 321–30.

standing as blameless before him (Eph 1:4), redemption, the forgiveness of sins (Eph 1:7), and an inheritance (Eph 1:11). This election, in time, brings about the proclamation of the gospel by which one is saved (Eph 1:13), and through faith the Holy Spirit is given (Eph 1:13–14).[16] Human salvation is initiated by God's grace, through which he resurrects dead sinners (Eph 2:1). God unites his people to Christ and grants them salvation apart from works (Eph 2:8–9). This text is particularly significant because it speaks about salvation apart from works in a general sense, and not simply works of Jewish law. The gospel excludes any human merit from justification.

There are several other texts which are relevant to the present discussions. One text which is of import is Philippians 3:1–11. In this text, Paul discusses his previous life as a Pharisee. Though he viewed himself as "blameless" under the law (Phil 3:6), he rejected all human righteousness when converting to the Christian faith. Salvation does not come as a result of human righteousness, but of God's righteousness which comes as a gift (Phil 3:9). One of the important truths expressed in this text is what David Hollaz refers to as the *unio fidei formalis*. Paul writes that he is "found in [Christ] not having my own righteousness, which is from the law, but that which is through faith in Christ" (Phil 3:9). Paul receives this righteousness precisely because he is *in Christ*. In other words, this union with Christ logically precedes justification, as it is the context in which God's righteousness is granted.[17] Thus there is a clear difference between the union by which passive righteousness is given and that by which the Christian grows in holiness.

There is not enough space in this work to adequately present all of the evidence that Paul viewed the Christian's life *coram Deo* as one of passive righteousness. This brief overview has, however, demonstrated that the theme of passive righteousness was developed through a thorough consideration of biblical texts; there is continuity between Paul and Luther on this subject.

---

16. Some scholastic Lutherans spoke of election as a conditional decree "in view of faith," whereas the Pauline argument presents faith itself as an effect of election. I discuss this controversy in Cooper, *Great Divide*, 6–9.

17. For a more thorough treatment of this text, see Vicars, *Jesus' Blood and Righteousness*, 205–11.

# Appendix

## Active Righteousness in Pauline Theology

There has been an extensive amount of Lutheran scholarship surrounding the nature of imputed righteousness and the veracity of justification *sola fide* in Paul's writings. Lutherans have not, however, spent as much effort in explaining the role of good works in Paul's theology and its relationship to the passive righteousness of faith. When examining the relevant texts, it is apparent that there is an intimate connection between faith and obedience, and that active righteousness is an essential aspect of the Christian's existence in this world.

We will begin our discussion with the book of Romans. As was demonstrated, the first five chapters of this epistle describe the inability of the law to save, as well as the nature of the gospel. In chapter six, Paul then begins a short discussion of Christian obedience. Paul presents a hypothetical interlocutor who asks, "What shall we say then? Shall we continue in sin that grace may abound?" (Rom 6:1). The concerns surrounding antinomianism are not new, but as ancient as the gospel itself. Paul anticipates that some people are going to question whether the free nature of the gospel gives one the right to live in sin. Interestingly, however, Paul does not immediately begin giving imperatives, but instead points back to the passive righteousness of faith. Paul argues that in baptism, the Christian is united to Christ's death and resurrection (Rom 6:3).[18] This, again, is the *unio fidei formalis*, whereby union with Christ establishes a reception of his benefits, including participation is his own death and resurrection. It is because of the reality of this passive righteousness in union with Christ that living in sin is now an impossibility for the Christian. For Paul, sanctification is rooted and grounded upon justification. Because one has been united to Christ in baptism, active righteousness must now be present in the Christian life. There is no talk of sanctification without the gospel at the center in Pauline thought. It is only after presenting the gospel reality of union with Christ that Paul gives the imperative, "Therefore, do not let sin reign in your mortal body, that you should obey it in its lust" (Rom 6:12). The gospel does not give the license to sin; it instead grants one the ability to live in righteousness.

The next extensive discussion of the Christian's obedience arises in chapter eight. It must be remembered that just prior to this discussion, Paul

18. "By so connecting us with Christ's death baptism so joined us to it that we ourselves died to sin. It was a dying together, this death of Christ and of ourselves, a being entombed together as dead" (Lenski, *Romans*, 393).

presents his ever-present struggle with indwelling sin, not to be completed prior to the eschaton. Thus, the battle between the old and new man is not negated by Romans 8, but instead, Paul presupposes it when beginning this discussion. Here, Paul speaks about the life that the believer has in the Spirit (Rom 8:1). The Christian is set free from the condemnation of the law, and having been set free, he now has an ability to begin to obey God's law (Rom 8:4). This life of sanctification is an eschatological reality, always pointing forward to the final day when sin is taken away. The same Spirit who raised Christ from the dead is at work within us, sanctifying us, and will one day grant us the gift of resurrection (Rom 8:11).

At one point in this section, Paul explicitly uses the language of righteousness (δικαίωμα) to refer to that which is done by the believer in accordance with God's law (Rom 8:2).[19] Paul is not suddenly forgetting the reality of forensic justification by grace to then place righteousness back into human performance. Not long after this, he speaks of righteousness as a forensic verdict by which one is "not guilty" because of the work of Christ (Rom 8:33). Paul can, instead, speak of righteousness in two different manners. In one perspective, righteousness is complete and imputed due to the righteousness of Christ. In the other, there is a righteousness that the Christian is called to live out as one is changed by God's Spirit. These two distinct righteousnesses have two distinct roles.

After an extensive discussion surrounding the role of Israel in redemptive history, Paul ends his epistle to the Romans with a number of commandments to guide the Roman congregation. This section begins in 12:1, wherein Paul urges them to present themselves to God as living sacrifices in view of the mercies of God. Paul draws upon the concept of eucharistic sacrifice here, demonstrating that good deeds are performed as acts of thanksgiving. Thus, the saving grace of God stands at the center of Christian obedience. Again, one's good deeds are performed in view of, and by the power of, the gospel.

Paul expounds upon several specific commandments, and nearly all of them are in reference to one's *coram mundo* relationships. In 12:3–8, Paul discusses the proper roles of Christians in the congregation. He then discusses the importance of giving to those in need (Rom 12:13), treating one another well (Rom 12:10), submitting to authority (Rom 13:1–7), bearing the burdens of others (Rom 15:1–6), and being sensitive to the weak in

---

19. "[W]e are changed, made alive unto God and delight in his holy will as this is voiced in his law" (Lenski, *Romans*, 497).

faith (Rom 14:1–13). Paul defines the law, which Christians should obey, by the love of neighbor (Rom 13:10). There is no indication in this text that these good works contribute to one's standing *coram Deo* or contribute to one's entrance into eternal glory. Instead, these good works are a necessary part of life in this world and in a Christian congregation. It is only after the free and full forgiveness of sins has been proclaimed that Paul then gives specific commandments; gospel assurance stands behind the Pauline imperatives.

The book of Galatians contains many of the same themes regarding active righteousness as does Romans. Paul presents the Christian life as one of liberty (Gal 5:1) through Christ. By faith, the Christian is justified and is set free from the penalty of God's law. This does not mean, however, that the Christian can live in sin. Paul urges the Galatians to use their liberty as an opportunity to serve one another, rather than giving into the sinful passions (Gal 5:13).[20] Here, as in Romans, Paul argues that love is the essence of the law that Christians are bound to obey (Gal 5:14). In light of this great commandment, Paul tells the Galatians to walk in the Spirit, and to avoid the works of the flesh (Gal 5:16–26). He is quick to point out that perfection is not expected, but that the Spirit and flesh battle against one another (Gal 5:16). The specific commandments given, again, are almost exclusively in reference to one's *coram mundo* relationships. It is only because one is in right relationship to God by passive righteousness that good deeds can be performed.

The book of Ephesians demonstrates a strong connection between active and passive righteousness. Immediately after proclaiming salvation by grace, Paul adds that "we are His workmanship, created in Christ Jesus for good works, which God prepared beforehand that we should walk in them" (Eph 2:10). God's predestinating action includes not only salvation, but also those good deeds that Christians will perform in this world. Paul is clear that one is not saved *by* these good works, but instead *for* these good works. Following this section, Paul further expounds upon the *coram mundo* aspects of Christian living, noting that just as Christ reconciled us to God the Father, so he also reconciled us to one another (Eph 2:14). Jew and Gentile are no longer at enmity with one another due to the work of Christ.

---

20. "The freedom of the Gospel does not permit a person to do as he pleases, does not sanction indulgence in sinful lusts. The liberty which the believers enjoy should rather be treated as an opening for loving service toward one another" (Kretzmann, *Popular Commentary* IV:253).

The book of Ephesians demonstrates a clear Christological emphasis within the Christian life. Paul notes that Christ indwells his people, and this indwelling is received by faith (Eph 3:17). This indwelling Christ is also instrumental in producing love within the hearts of God's people (Eph 3:17–19). Paul speaks not only of what God has done *for* us, but of what he is effecting *in* us (Eph 3:20). Paul's forensic soteriological emphasis does not negate a strong doctrine of union with Christ and divine indwelling.[21] There is a type of Christ-mysticism found in Pauline theology, wherein God's indwelling conforms the believer to Christ's image, and one is filled with the "fullness of God" (Eph 3:19).[22] This is what the Lutheran scholastic tradition referred to as the *unio mystica*. As was demonstrated above, at times Paul connects union with Christ to the reception of God's righteousness (e.g., in Phil 3:9); here and in other texts, however, Paul utilizes union language in connection to the sanctifying indwelling of Christ's person in the believer. Both aspects of union with Christ explained by Hollaz and the subsequent Lutheran tradition are thoroughly Pauline.

As do Romans and Galatians, Ephesians demonstrates a pastoral focus for Paul. He speaks about the importance of each believer's role *coram mundo* within the realm of the church (Eph 4:7–16). Each Christian serves a different function as do different parts of one's human body. This Christian life involves the putting off of the old man and the putting on of the new, which in Pauline theology is symbolic of the sinful and renewed aspects of the human person (Eph 4:22–24). The putting on of the new self consists primarily in showing love to one's neighbor, in view of the love God demonstrates in Christ (Eph 5:2). This love is shown through ordinary earthly activities, such as one working with one's hands (Eph 5:28), a wife submitting to her husband (Eph 5:22), a husband loving his wife (Eph 5:25), children obeying their parents (Eph 6:2), and a master treating his slave well (Eph 6:9). Each of the imperatives in Ephesians is connected to one's earthly vocation, demonstrating a clear horizontal emphasis in Christian living. This horizontal life of service to one's neighbor in each of life's

---

21. "Not only the gifts and virtues of Christ, but the exalted Christ personally lives in the hearts of His believers, Gal. 2, 20. There is the most intimate, the most happy communion between Christ and the Christians, begun in conversion, but in need of daily growth and strengthening, for it is through faith that Christ dwells in the heart, and the loss of faith in the forgiveness of sins means the loss of Christ Himself . . . But with Christ in the heart, there is steady progress" (Kretzmann, *Popular Commentary*, IV:274–75).

22. See my discussion of this topic in Cooper, *Christification*, 48–72.

stations is only possible due to the union that Christ has with each believer in faith.

Lutherans have sometimes presented a truncated Paulinism, in which the indicatives of the Pauline epistles override any essential import of the latter halves of his writings. Steven Paulson's book *Lutheran Theology*, for example, portrays itself as a loose commentary on the book of Romans. Yet, the book focuses almost exclusively on the texts pertaining to sin and justification, giving relatively little space to the important ethical issues addressed by Paul in Romans 12–16. Too often in Lutheran preaching, when the imperative Pauline texts appear in the lectionary, the preacher chooses to expound upon the gospel lesson in order to avoid giving concise and distinct ethical commands to the congregation for fear of moralism. With the two-kids-of-righteousness framework, these texts can be understood properly, and proclaimed honestly, without any need to explain away every imperative text as simply an example of the second use of the law.

## Active and Passive Righteousness in the Book of James

It is well known that the book of James was labeled by Luther an "epistle of straw"[23] and has been at the center of the controversy between the Roman Catholic and Lutheran positions on the nature of justification. Because of this fact, some Lutherans may not preach on this epistle, and it receives a relatively small amount of attention in comparison with the other books in the New Testament from Lutheran authors and pastors. Within the two-kinds-of-righteousness framework, however, the Epistle of James is perfectly consistent with the rest of Scripture in proclaiming the free nature of the gospel alongside of the necessity of good deeds performed for the sake of the neighbor.

While it might seem at first glance as if James focuses solely on active righteousness, he does in fact portray one's relationship to God as one of passivity. God is portrayed as the giver of all good things, and he does this liberally (Jas 1:5). Man's stance before God is one of faith, through which he receives from the Lord (Jas 1:6–7). James further argues that all good things in this life are gifts of the Heavenly Father (Jas 1:17). These gifts include regeneration, which is the result of God's will and the divine word (Jas 1:18).[24] In his discussion of the mistreatment of the poor within the

23. *Works of Martin Luther* VI:477–79.

24. "With his description of the Christian's birth from God by the Word, James is

Christian community, James speaks of God's election of the poor, which includes the gift of faith and inheritance of the kingdom of God (Jas 2:5). James also continually speaks of humility before God. Through acknowledging the reality of sin and humbling oneself before God, one is exalted by grace (Jas 4:10). All of this is perfectly consistent with the passive nature of *coram Deo* righteousness.

James further acknowledges the universal nature of human sinfulness, even among Christians. Prior to beginning his discussion regarding the relationship between the tongue and sinful speech, James confesses that "we all stumble in many things" (Jas 3:2). James follows this statement by arguing that if one does not stumble in words, he is a perfect man (Jas 3:2). Since James just stated that we do in fact stumble, it is apparent that such a perfect man does not exist, aside from the person of Jesus himself. In the beginning of chapter four, the reality of sin in the Christian life is even more apparent, as James confronts his readers as "adulterers and adulteresses!" (Jas 4:4). He then assures his readers that despite their sin, God's grace is sufficient to forgive and exalt them through repentance (Jas 4:6).

In view of this previous discussion, James' controversial section in chapter two can be explained in a manner which is consistent with his contention that one's relationship to God is passive, that sin is a continual reality in the Christian life, and that God's grace exalts all who repent. In chapter two, James discusses the relationship between faith and works in the Christian life. This discussion begins with James asking about the usefulness of faith if there are no works flowing from the faithful person (Jas 2:14). James argues that this faith—one that exists without works—is not saving. This is perfectly consistent with the historic Lutheran contention about the necessity of good deeds. James simply says that a works-less faith does not save, not that works somehow *make* faith saving. As is demonstrated in the same chapter, works serve an evidential purpose. As James writes, "I will show you my faith by my works" (Jas 2:18). Works serve to demonstrate the reality of faith.

Though some contemporary interpreters speak about a "second justification" before God based on works, the context makes it apparent that the justification spoken of here has nothing to do with salvation at

touching the doctrines of the sacraments, the Holy Spirit, and authority. This act of birth in their baptism is at the foundation of his readers' lives. Through God's act of begetting in baptism they have come into a new relationship with Him" (Scaer, *James*, 60).

all; rather, James speaks of justification *coram mundo.*[25] This epistle speaks extensively of the nature of relationships between members of the body of Christ. He admonishes those who treat the rich and the poor differently (Jas 2:1–4), those who judge others unrighteously (Jas 2:11–12), and the rich who value their wealth more than others, whom they murder (Jas 5:1–6). Because the text deals so extensively with *coram mundo* relational issues, it is plausible that justification would be explained in this context. Immediately preceding his statement that "faith without works is dead," James gives an example of the uselessness of faith without works. He mentions a circumstance in which someone needs food, and one gives kind words without actually giving something to satisfy that person's hunger. In this context, the neighbor is not actually served. Similarly, faith without works is useless, because without works, the neighbor is not served. In the *coram mundo* realm, then, it is true that one is justified, or "vindicated," by works, and not by faith alone. James is simply not utilizing justification language in the soteriological sense as Paul does.

## Conclusion

Ultimately, any theological development must be founded upon the biblical text and not just any particular theological tradition. Though this work is primarily a historical theological one, this appendix hopefully demonstrates that this theme is ultimately rooted in Holy Scripture. This treatment is only cursory, and I did not even discuss the relevant texts from the gospels, the general epistles, or most of the Old Testament books. Hopefully future work on this subject will do so in more depth than is possible from a historical and systematic theologian. Even a short treatment, however, demonstrates that Holy Scripture clearly and continually explains the free nature of salvation in Christ and the necessity of holy living in accordance with God's law. These two realities are most clearly proclaimed and distinguished by the two-kinds-of-righteousness framework.

---

25. There has been a significant amount of controversy in the Reformed community surrounding Norman Shepherd's idea of a second justification based on works, along with a definition of faith which includes works within it. See, for example, his book *The Call of Grace.* This idea has been utilized in many Federal Vision writings and bears some similarity to the doctrine of justification in New Perspective writers.

# Bibliography

Alexander, Donald. *Christian Spirituality: Five Views of Sanctification.* Downers Grove, IL: Intervarsity, 1989.

Arand, Charles. "Two Kinds of Righteousness as a Framework for Law and Gospel in the Apology." *Lutheran Quarterly* XV/4 (2001) 417–39.

Arand, Charles P. and Joel Biermann. "Why the Two Kinds of Righteousness?" *Concordia Journal* 33/2 (2007) 116–35.

Arand, Charles P., Robert Kolb, and James A. Nestingen. *The Lutheran Confessions: History and Theology of the Book of Concord.* Minneapolis: Fortress, 2012.

Barth, Karl. *The Word of God and the Word of Man.* Translated by Douglas Horton. New York: Harper & Row, 1957.

Bartsch, Hans Werner. *Kerygma and Myth: Rudolf Bultmann & Five Critics.* New York: Harper, 1961.

Bayer, Oswald. *Living by Faith: Justification and Sanctification.* Translated by Geoffrey W. Bromily. Grand Rapids: Eerdmans, 2003.

———. *Theology the Lutheran Way.* Translated by Jeffrey G. Silcock and Mark C. Mattes. Grand Rapids: Eerdmans, 2007.

Biermann, Joel D. *A Case for Character: Towards a Lutheran Virtue Ethics.* Minneapolis: Fortress, 2014.

Bolt, John. "Why the Covenant of Works Is a Necessary Doctrine" In *By Faith Alone: Answering the Challenges to the Doctrine of Justification*, 171–190 edited by Gary L.W. Johnson, and Guy P. Waters. Wheaton, IL: Crossway, 2007.

Braaten, Carl E. and Robert W. Jenson, eds. *Christian Dogmatics.* Vols. 1 and 2. Philadelphia: Fortress, 2011.

———. *Union with Christ: The New Finnish Interpretation of Luther.* Grand Rapids: Eerdmans, 1998.

Calvin, John. *Institutes of the Christian Religion.* Translated by John T. McNeil. Louisville: Westminster John Knox, 1960.

Carson, D.A., Peter T. O'Brien, and Mark A. Seifrid, editors. *Justification and Variegated Nomism.* 2 vols. Grand Rapids: Baker, 2001, 2004.

Cooper, Jordan. *Christification: A Lutheran Approach to Theosis.* Eugene, OR: Wipf and Stock, 2014.

———. *The Great Divide: A Lutheran Evaluation of Reformed Theology.* Eugene, OR: Wipf and Stock, 2015.

———. *The Righteousness of One: An Evaluation of Early Patristic Soteriology in Light of the New Perspective on Paul.* Eugene, OR: Wipf and Stock, 2013.

# Bibliography

Dennison, William D. *The Young Bultmann: Context for his Understanding of God 1884–1935*. New York: Peter Lang, 2008.

Elam, Andrew M. *Merit and Moses: A Critique of the Klinean Doctrine of Republication*. Eugene, OR: Wipf and Stock, 2014.

Elert, Werner. *The Structure of Lutheranism*. Translated by Walter A. Hansen. St. Louis: Concordia, 1962.

Forde, Gerhard O. *A More Radical Gospel: Essays on Eschatology, Authority, Atonement, and Ecumenism*. Edited by Mark C. Mattes and Steven D. Paulson. Grand Rapids: Eerdmans, 2004.

———. *Justification by Faith: A Matter of Life and Death*. Mifflintown, PA: Sigler, 1990.

———. *Where God Meets Man: Luther's Down to Earth Approach to the Gospel*. Minneapolis: Augsburg, 1972.

Frame, John R. *Systematic Theology*. Phillipsburg, NJ: P&R, 2013.

Franzmann, Martin H. *The Word of the Lord Grows: An Introduction to the Origin, Purpose, and Meaning of the New Testament*. St. Louis: Concordia, 1961.

Gerberding, George Henry. *The Way of Salvation in the Lutheran Church*. Philadelphia: General Council, 1918.

Gerhard, Johann. *Sacred Meditations*. Translated by Wade R. Johnston. Saginaw, MI: Publisher, 2011.

Gritsch, Eric W. *A History of Lutheranism*. Minneapolis: Fortress, 2002.

Grobien, Gifford. "Righteousness, Mystical Union, and Moral Formation in Christian Worship." *Concordia Theological Quarterly* 77/1–2 (2013): 141–64.

Hauerwas, Stanley. *Hannah's Child: A Theologian's Memoir*. Grand Rapids: Eerdmans, 2010.

Horton, Michael S. *The Christian Faith: A Systematic Theology of the Christian Faith*. Grand Rapids: Zondervan, 2011.

Jacobs, Henry Eyster. *A Summary of the Christian Faith*. Philadelphia: General Council, 1907.

———. *Elements of Religion*. Philadelphia: General Council, 1913.

Kline, Meredith. *Kingdom Prologue: Genesis Foundations for a Covenant Worldview*. Eugene: Wipf & Stock, 2006.

Kolb, Robert and Timothy J. Wengert, eds. *The Book of Concord: The Confessions of the Evangelical Lutheran Church*. Translated by Charles Arand et. al. Minneapolis: Fortress, 2000.

Kolb, Robert and Charles P. Arand. *The Genius of Luther's Theology: A Wittenberg Way of Thinking for the Contemporary Church*. Grand Rapids: Baker, 2008.

Kolb, Robert. "God and His Human Creatures in Luther's Sermons on Genesis: The Reformer's Early Use of His Distinction of Two Kinds of Righteousness." *Concordia* 33/2 (2007) 166–84.

———. "Luther on the Two Kinds of Righteousness; Reflections on His Two-Dimensional Definition of Humanity at the Heart of His Theology." *Lutheran Quarterly* XIII/4 (1999) 449–66.

Kretzmann, Paul E. *Popular Commentary of the Bible*. 4 vols. St. Louis: Concordia, 1923.

Lenski, R.C.H. *The Interpretation of St. Paul's Epistle to the Romans*. Minneapolis: Augsburg, 1961.

Lindberg, Conrad Emil. *Christian Dogmatics and Notes on the History of Dogma*. Rock Island, IL: Augustana, 1922.

# Bibliography

Lund, Eric. *Documents from the History of Lutheranism 1517–1750*. Minneapolis: Fortress, 2002.

Luther, Martin. *Lectures on Galatians Chapters 1–4*. Edited by Jarislav Pelikan. Vol. 26 of *Luther's Works*. Saint Louis: Concordia, 1963.

———. *Lectures on Galatians Chapters 5–6*. Edited by Jarislav Pelikan. Vol. 27 of *Luther's Works*. Saint Louis: Concordia, 1964.

———. *Career of the Reformer I*. Edited by Harold J. Grimm and Helmut T. Lehmann. Vol. 31 of *Luther's Works*. Philadelphia: Fortress, 1957.

———. *Career of the Reformer II*. Edited by George W. Forell and Helmut T. Lehmann. Vol. 32 of *Luther's Works*. Philadelphia: Fortress, 1958.

———. *Career of the Reformer III*. Edited by Watson, Philip S. Vol. 33 of *Luther's Works*. Philadelphia: Fortress, 1968.

———. *Career of the Reformer IV*. Edited by Lewis William Spitz and Helmut T. Lehmann. Vol. 34 of *Luther's Works*. Philadelphia: Fortress, 1968.

———. *Works of Martin Luther Vol. IV*. Philadelphia: Muhlenberg, 1931.

———. *Only the Decalogue Is Eternal: Martin Luther's Complete Antimonian Disputations*. Edited and translated by Holger Sonntag. Minneapolis: Luther Press, 2008.

Macquarrie, John. *An Existentialist Theology: A Comparison of Heidegger and Bultmann*. New York: Harper, 1960.

Mannermaa, Tuomo. *Christ Present in Faith: Luther's View of Justification*. Edited by Kirsi I. Stjerna. Minneapolis: Fortress, 2005.

Marquart, Kurt. "Luther and Theosis." *Concordia Theological Quarterly* 64/3 (2000) 182–205.

Martensen, Hans. *Christian Dogmatics*. Edinburgh: T&T Clark, 1898.

Middendorf, Michael P. *The "I" in the Storm: A Study of Romans 7*. St. Louis: Concordia, 1997.

Mildenberger, Friedrich. *Theology of the Lutheran Confessions*. Translated by Erwin Lueker. Philadelphia: Fortress, 1986.

Murray, Scott R. *Law, Life, and the Living God: The Third Use of the Law in Modern American Lutheranism*. Saint Louis: Concordia, 2001.

Oliphant, Scott K. *Justified in Christ: God's Plan for Us in Justification*. London: Mentor, 2001.

Paulson, Steven D. *Lutheran Theology*. New York: T&T Clark, 2011.

Pieper, Franz. *Christian Dogmatics*. 4 Vols. Saint Louis: Concordia, 1950–1957.

Preus, Robert D. *A Contemporary Look at the Formula of Concord*. St. Louis: Concordia, 1978.

Remensnyder, Junius Benjamin. *The Lutheran Manual*. New York: Boschen and Wefer, 1893.

Roehrs, Walter R. *Survey of Covenant History: A Historical Overview of the Old Testament*. St. Louis: Concordia, 1989.

Saleska, Timothy. "The Two Kinds of Righteousness! What's a Preacher to Do?" *Concordia* 33/2 (2007) 136–45.

Scaer, David P. *James, the Apostle of Faith: A Primary Christological Epistle for the Persecuted Church*. Eugene, OR: Wipf and Stock, 1994.

Schlink, Edmund. *Theology of the Lutheran Confessions*. Translated by Paul F. Koehneke. Saint Louis: Concordia, 1961.

Schmauk, Theodore E. and C. Theodore Benze. *The Confessional Principle and the Confessions of the Lutheran Church*. Saint Louis: Concordia, 2005.

Schmid, Heinrich. *The Doctrinal Theology of the Evangelical Lutheran Church*. Translated by Charles A. Hay and Henry Eyster Jacobs. Minneapolis: Augsburg, 1875.

Shepherd, Norman. *The Call of Grace: How the Covenant Illuminates Salvation and Evangelism*. Phillipsburg, NJ: Presbyterian and Reformed, 2002.

Stump, Joseph. *The Christian Faith: A System of Christian Dogmatics*. Philadelphia: Muhlenberg, 1942.

Vickers, Brian. *Jesus' Blood and Righteousness: Paul's Theology of Imputation*. Wheaton, IL: Crossway, 2006.

Voigt, Andrew George. *Biblical Dogmatics*. Columbia, SC: Lutheran Board of Publication, 1917.

Walther, C. F. W. *Selected Sermons*. Watseka, IL: Just and Sinner, 2014.

Weidner, Revere Franklin. *Biblical Theology of the Old Testament*. Rock Island, IL: Augustana, 1896.

———. *Christian Ethics: A System Based on Martensen and Harless*. New York: Flemming H. Revel, 1891.

———. *Pneumatology: Or the Doctrine Concerning the Holy Spirit*. Chicago: Wartburg, 1915.

Wenthe, Dean O. "The *Torah* Story: Identity or Duty as the Essence of the Law" In *The Law in Holy Scripture*, edited by Charles A. Gieschen, 21–36. St. Louis: Concordia, 2004.

Westerholm, Stephen. *Perspectives Old and New on Paul: The "Lutheran" Paul and His Critics*. Grand Rapids: Eerdmans, 2004.

Wingren, Gustaf. *Creation and Law*. Translated by Ross MacKenzie. Eugene, OR: Wipf and Stock, 2003.

———. *Luther on Vocation*. Translated by Carl C. Rasmussen. Philadelphia: Muhlenberg, 1957.

Winter, Lincoln. "Law and Gospel Are Good Enough for Me." *Musings of a Country Person* (blog). November 28, 2011. https://predigtamt.wordpress.com/2011/11/28/law-and-gospel-are-good-enough-for-me/.

Wubbenhorst, Karla. "Calvin's Doctrine of Justification: Variations on a Lutheran Theme." In *Justification in Perspective: Historical Developments and Contemporary Challenges*, edited by Bruce L. McCormack, 99–118. Grand Rapids: Baker, 2006.

Made in the USA
Columbia, SC
16 February 2018